Further praise for *Maggie & Me*:

'Full to the brim with poignancy, humour, brutality and energetic and sometimes shimmering prose . . . It is hugely affecting' *Sunday Times*

'A nuanced, subtle and original account . . . a memoir which is both personally moving and a valuable historical document' *Literary Review*

'*Maggie & Me* by Damian Barr has a startling new take on the former PM' *Herald*

'Few writers can wind you with a word. But Damian Barr doesn't just do that, he tickles and then floors you, delights only to devastate, within a single phrase . . . I won't be happy until everyone reads this book' Patrick Strudwick

'An inspiring read' *Marie Claire*

'This book will break your heart and make you angry; then it will lift your heart and make you glad; because Damian Barr has transmuted a grim childhood into a work of art and brought forth beauty from ashes' Richard Holloway

'Witty, gritty and inspiring' *Glamour*

'*Maggie & Me* is a refreshing, affecting and ultimately triumphant account of growing up in the shadow of the Iron Lady' *Metro*

'I was dazzled by the energy and verve of Damian Barr's memoir . . . I've been shoving copies into people's hands all year' *Evening Standard* Bool

'Admiringly deadpan . . . Barr captures very well how it is possible to learn and to love even in the most unpropitious environment. His book is the better for the strange loyalty it shows to the place he fled' Charles Moore, *Daily Telegraph*

'Brilliantly observed, searingly intimate and painfully truthful, *Maggie & Me* brought the eighties back to me at the same time as making me question my established views of the whole decade. In other words, like the very best books, it changed me a little' Sathnam Sanghera

'A gifted storyteller, weaving skilfully back and forth through time, and his unfussy prose flows delightfully . . . This vibrant language roots his story firmly in a west of Scotland . . . Splendid' *Independent on Sunday*

'This memoir of deprivation and survival is shrewdly constructed and written with a winning dry humour' *Guardian*

'Fond, funny, involving and at times emotionally wrenching' *Sunday Times*

'Easily my favourite book of 2013 . . . Of all the biographies and memoirs of the great woman this is the most unusual and the most profound . . . There isn't a trace of bitterness in the beautiful book. Only the radiant eloquence of a man whose courage and humanity shine from its pages' Alan Johnson, *New Statesman* Books of the Year

Maggie & Me

DAMIAN BARR has been a journalist for over ten years, writing mostly for *The Times* but also the *Independent, Telegraph, Financial Times, Guardian, Evening Standard* and *Granta*. He is the author of *Get It Together: A Guide to Surviving Your Quarterlife Crisis*, featured on *Richard & Judy*, and has co-written two plays for BBC Radio 4. He is a Fellow of the Royal Society of Arts, Faculty at the School of Life and host of his own infamous Literary Salon. He was Stonewall's Writer of the Year in 2013 and lives in Brighton.

Follow him on Twitter @Damian_Barr

Maggie & Me

Damian Barr

BLOOMSBURY
LONDON · NEW DELHI · NEW YORK · SYDNEY

Bloomsbury Publishing Plc
50 Bedford Square
London
WC1B 3DP

www.bloomsbury.com

Bloomsbury is a trade mark of Bloomsbury Publishing Plc

Bloomsbury Publishing, London, New Delhi, New York and Sydney
A CIP catalogue record for this book is available from the British Library

ISBN 978 1 4088 3809 9

10 9 8 7 6 5 4 3 2 1

Typeset by Hewer Text Uk Ltd, Edinburgh

Printed and bound in Great Britain by CPI Group (UK) Ltd, Croydon CR0 4YY

For Mike

'Of course it's the same old story. Truth usually is the same old story.'

Margaret Thatcher,
Prime Minister's Questions, 1990

INTRODUCTION

'Britain needs an Iron Lady.'
Margaret Thatcher, Speech to Conservative Rally,
Birmingham, 19 April 1979

IT'S THE 12TH OF October 1984. I am just eight years old. Me and my mum are stuck to the *BBC Nine O'Clock News* in this strange new flat. We sit cross-legged on bare floorboards with coats for cushions and watch ambulances, police cars and fire engines mee-maw, mee-maw in black-and-white on the portable balancing on top of a tea chest. A flurry of dusty black bits fluttered out when I helped my mum turn it upside down. I thought tea only came in bags until this morning when the removal van came to take us to Flat 1, 1 Magdalene Drive, Carfin. My dad is back at 25 Ardgour Place, Newarthill with the big colour telly. My wee sister, Teenie, has cried herself to sleep in my mum's lap. Our old life is crammed in the cardboard boxes bursting all around us. It's way past my bedtime but rules are already being broken.

My mum lifts an arm so I can snuggle in. She lights a Regal cigarette and shakes her head at the telly, tutting and pulling me closer. I can't get close enough. Blue smoke cloaks us.

'Luck o' the devil,' she huffs, puffing away at the telly where this blonde woman rises from rubble again and again like a Cyberman off *Doctor Who*.

All around her the hotel is collapsing as bloody bodies are pulled out but she stays calm. She's talking to the BBC with a man's voice and even the police stop to listen. 'Life must go on as usual,' she insists, as if life will do exactly what she tells it.

'Shit disnae burn, Maggie won't,' says my mum, smoking at the portable, puffing extra fast, super deep like it's a race. I look up at her with questioning eyes. We shouldn't be here. 'He disnae like them, "cancer sticks", he calls them,' she confides, smoothing Teenie's blonde bobbed hair with her free hand, her nails chewed to nothing.

He is Logan and according to all the arguments I've overheard, he's the man my mum is leaving my dad for. Right now he's asleep in the next room because plumbers start early. We're not to wake him. He was waiting for us in the empty flat when we arrived with all our boxes. Not as tall as my dad but not as short as my mum, he stood totally still filling every room so we could hardly breathe. Without a word he handed her a key then pushed his face into hers.

'The weans,' she whispered, blushing and shuffling.

He looked down at Teenie then me, his mouth open, lips red like inside a cut. I held her hand tight and all the lines round everything sharpened. I breathed right in.

'So ah see,' he said slowly, before whipping a Stanley knife from the pocket of his blue boiler suit and slashing the top of a box. 'Ah'm Logan.'

The telly was first to get unpacked. The News was already on when Logan plugged it in. He thumped it hard just once and the picture cleared to show Maggie walking away from the bombed hotel. He shook his head and changed the channel but there she was again. Nine hours of unpacking later and the News is still on and Maggie's still not dead. He can't believe it. Neither can my mum. They hate her and they say she hates Scotland, hates us. But all the people on the BBC seem glad she made it. Secretly, I am too. I don't want to see her dead. I don't know why – maybe just because everybody else does. She's not done anything to me. I'd like to brush the dust from her big blonde hair like she's a Girl's World and tell her it'll all be all right. Of course, I can't admit this.

'Bitch,' I say, the worst word I know, and flinch for a skelp.

But my mum says nothing, not even a 'God forgive you'. So I'm allowed to swear about Maggie. That's how bad she is.

My mum takes one last puff. I don't want her to go and sleep in that bed with him. I close my eyes as she drops her cigarette hissing into the dregs of a cuppa and imagine celebrating Maggie's miraculous escape with the shiny rich-looking people on the telly.

The Grand Hotel survives. So does Maggie. So will I.

'There are individual men and women and there are families and no government can do anything except through people and people look to themselves first. It is our duty to look after ourselves and then also to help look after our neighbour . . . There is no such thing as society.'

Margaret Thatcher, *Woman's Own*,
23 September 1987

'I T'S TIME TO PLAY the music, it's time to light the lights,' sings the big colour telly from downstairs at 25 Ardgour Place, Newarthill.

'Mum, it's *The Muppet Show*!' I jiggle as she stretches the towel between her arms ready to wrap me up tight before carrying me downstairs, a ritual I am 'getting too big and too old for' but which is still allowed if my dad's out at work. 'We'll miss Kermit!' I squeal, bursting through the brown-and-orange towel like a finishing line, across the cork floor towards the stairs.

'Damian Leighton Barr, what have I told you about running in the house!' The dreaded middle name only ever used when I'm in trouble.

Her words wrap around me with the towel as she scoops me up, carrying me down into the living room where the curtain is going up on our most favourite programme in the whole world ever.

'It's time to put on make-up, it's time to dress up right, it's time to get things started!' We sing along. I'm sitting on her lap cocooned in the towel, part of the set she boil-washes in Acdo every Sunday morning in the thundering twin-tub that she pulls out from under the scullery sink. They were a wedding present, she warns whenever I drop one on the floor. It's my job to hand her the big wooden tongs for fishing things out when it's stopped spinning.

Kermit announces that this week's special guest is Superman! Christopher Reeve's kiss curl smooches his forehead and me and my mum gasp.

'You love that Superman, don't you, son?'

I nod and leap off her lap and fly round naked, the towel is my cape. 'D-D-D DA DA DAH! D-D-D DA DA DAH!' I do the theme and land in her lap just in time to hear a key in the back door. Can it be? Is that my dad home early from the Craig? Are all the best things in the world happening at once? My head spins as my mum picks me up by the shoulders and stands me on the carpet, eyeing the sunburst clock that ticks over the electric fire where both bars burn because it's bath night and she knows I like it roasty-toasty.

'Daaaaaaaaaad!' I zoom at him Superman-style, one arm out front, the other by my side, hitting the cold air he brings in from outside. My dad is always minerals. The whites of his eyes and his smiling falsers sparkle out from the coal-black rest of him.

My mum chunters, 'Ocht, Glenn, the wean's just had his bath!' but she's too late to stop me getting dirty and I don't really think she wants to anyway.

I'm flying up in the sky, dipping and diving and soaring and swooping, the living-room carpet swirling brown and orange far below me. My dad has superpowers.

'How's ma Superboy?' he asks, grizzling in to kiss the back of my neck.

The stubble that's grown in on his twelve-hour shift tickles and he nuzzles me harder and I squeal and he doesn't stop and suddenly I can't feel his hands holding me any more and I'm hurtling towards the couch hundreds of miles below and then . . . 'Got ye!' I'm back in his gigantic hands. He'd planned it all along!

My mum stands, hands on her narrow hips, and pretends to disapprove when he produces two Strawberry Mivvis from the pocket of his donkey jacket. She is five foot nothing. He is six foot everything. She buzzes like a bee in a jar.

'Yous'll have tae brush yer teeth again!' He laughs, popping his false teeth out and rolling his eyes. We shriek like we always do.

Mum smile-tuts at my dad. 'An' you,' she says pointing upstairs. 'Time for yer bath.'

My pram is parked in the corner of the living room and I know it was mine because I remember lying in it looking out through the frothy lace fringe at faces smiling in. I remember bouncing along the pavement.

'Yer daddy wis the only man that pushed a pram in the whole village,' my mum boasts. 'He took you round and round the scheme. He wis that proud.'

I wasn't the first one in the pram. There was someone in it before me. A girl.

'Heaven,' says Granny Mac when I ask where she went, turning her head away from me with chopping-onions eyes. 'Wit's fur yae disnae go by yae.'

6

This is her favourite expression along with 'Least said, soonest mended', 'Fly wi the craws ye get shot wi the craws', 'Hell mend yae', 'Jesus, Mary and Joseph', 'Aw fur coat and nae knickers', and 'Don't come runnin' tae me' as in 'Damian Leighton Barr, if you fall off that wall and break your leg don't come runnin' tae me!' So I don't ask again.

Soon the navy-blue Silver Cross pram with its prim white wheels will be rolling out again. Not with me because I'm getting to be a big boy now, already taking after my dad and only four. Nearly five! I tug on my blue-leather reins trying to get ahead.

'Damy, ye'll pull me over,' my mum warns.

Women stop her in the Fine Fayre and ask if she puts me to bed in a Grobag. I'm nearly at her waist already.

'You'll have a wee sister soon,' my mum says when I ask her why she looks so fat. 'She's in here,' she explains, patting her moon belly, letting me in on the secret as usual.

I wonder how she got in there and how she'll get out and what will happen to me when she does.

Technically bedtime is 7 p.m. But if my dad is still at the Craig I am allowed to stay up. Even if I'm tired – which I never am – my mum snuggles me next to her on the couch 'for the company'. Sometimes she reads out loud from her Mills & Boons, sounding out all the words, even the ones I don't understand. She cuts out the headlines from the *Daily Record* and we turn the letters into words and the words into stories. I learn that nurses always fancy doctors and a broken heart always heals. If she's too tired to read we watch the telly.

Our telly has fancy faux teak trimmings and it smells burny when you clunk it on because the stour that gathers beyond my mum's duster in the vents at the back singes as the valves warm up. She wrinkles her tiny freckled nose at the smell, every time. Thanks to my dad's bulging Friday pay packet from the Craig we've got the only colour telly on Ardgour Place. We can watch three channels in a thousand colours. Two men from the Cooperative Department Store in Motherwell carry it in just in time for the Royal Wedding, which is taking attention away from my birthday.

'Wit a meringue!' says my mum when she sees Lady Di's dress.

'You'd no fill the front,' laughs Auntie Louisa, my mum's only sister in a band of six brothers.

She gets a look from Granny Mac who sounds out her name 'Lou-eez-a' while fingering her rosary.

My dad looks bored. St Paul's Cathedral looks like a giant Tunnock's Tea Cake. It's bigger than the church and the chapel put together and Granny Mac nods approvingly. It's full of hats.

'Oh look at the state of her,' says my mum, pointing.

Auntie Louisa and Granny Mac tut as one. Even my dad sits up a bit.

'That Maggie's dressed fer a funeral. Black, at a weddin''.'

Me and my mum have a strict telly diet of hot sweet tea, a Tunnock's Tea Cake or two, salt and vinegar crisps and *Hart to Hart*. Like all Americans, Mr and Mrs Hart look rich. Every week they fight crime with big hair and wall-to-wall teeth even whiter than my dad's falsers. The Harts speed along seaside roads in a wee red car that my dad knows the name of and never mess a hair on their heads. They're always at glittering parties where sparkling drinks are brought in tall glasses on silver trays by black men. Ahmed, whose parents own the Paki shop, is the closest thing to black round here.

Mr Hart is always polite, even to the black men, and flame-haired Mrs Hart has a flirty smile for everybody. They even have a servant: Max. Mr Hart made all his millions himself, which makes them even better. Mrs Hart is a fiery redhead journalist. Max says she's 'goy-jus'. She is. Right there and then I decide to be a journalist when I grow up: solving mysteries, meeting famous people and occasionally tapping at a typewriter before walking into the sunset laughing with my own Mr Hart.

My mum wants to be Mrs Hart and I do too but she can't grow her hair out because it goes too curly. 'At least mine's natural,' she says. That's how my dad knew she was a Catholic. She was leaving school with no O levels and he was already working at the Craig. 'He was that handsome, yer daddy,' she says. 'Handsomer than Mr Hart. Still is. But yer Granny Mac was not happy and neither was yer Granny Barr.' She looks at the rings on her fingers.

'Jet-setters,' says my mum wistfully, carefully unwrapping a Tea Cake so she doesn't dent or crack the perfect chocolate dome beneath. 'Money folk.'

It's 1981. No one in my family has been on a plane. My mum went to 'that Belgium' for Kitty Smith's wedding to a Flemish man called Pieter. She went on a train and a ferry 'without yer daddy' and ate '*moules* – "worse than whelks"' and laughed at a statue of a wee boy peeing and bought an ornament of an old man selling balloons which I've got to mind when I am playing. None of the rest of us has been further than Glasgow.

In every episode Mr and Mrs Hart solve thefts and murders which Max pronounces 'moy-duh'. Often the corpse or culprit is sniffed out by Freeway the dog. He's called Freeway because the Harts rescued him from the roadside. I fantasise about finding a puppy beside the road that goes from Mother-well to Glasgow, where my dad took us to see the Christmas lights in George Square. 'M8' doesn't sound quite as good. Anyway, the doctor says I'm allergic to cats and dogs.

My wee mum is getting bigger like she's been at the Tun-nock's. My dad kids on that he can't lift her and she shoos him away.

'Not long now, son,' she says, patting her belly and looking at the pram.

Our neighbours on one side are the Browns. Mr and Mrs Brown have had white hair for ever and a grown-up son called William with hair so thick and black you can't see his scalp. I spend hours at my bedroom window staring down at the top of his head while he lies out on the one sunny day that year. All three of them go out to work every day. I never see them mow their lawn but it's never any longer than my pinkie. A hedge of yellow roses grows round it and this summer I pushed my hand through the fence and nicked some to mix with water to make 'perfume'. My mum said it smelled lovely.

'Stunning whites.' My mum envies Mrs Brown's brand-new automatic washing machine. 'Her twin-tub's gone the journey,' she says, crossing herself.

On the other side are the Connors, all eight of them burst-ing out a three-bedroomed house the same as ours. 'You'd think the Council would move them up,' says my mum. She'd hate it if they flitted, no more mid-morning cuppa with Leena ('only the priest calls me Coleen').

My dad would love them to be anywhere but next door. Leena and Gerry don't work, they're probably too busy looking after Bernadette, Mary, Brendan, Sean, Aileen and Danny. 'Bloody Catholics,' my dad says and his bloody Catholic wife jumps up to clout him. That's his last word on religion.

Danny is only about my age but Bernadette, the oldest, is already at Taylor High School. She's got a turn in her eye so you never know where she's looking. Our back garden has a green for drying washing and a pebble-dashed concrete shed same as everybody else's in the Gas Scheme. Ardgour Place is part of the Gas Scheme, which means we've got central heating. We don't have a chimney, not like the Coal Scheme where Granny Mac stays. She doesn't trust gas, says it's a dry heat and pats her chest.

The Connors have paved their back garden and turned it into a zoo. They've not got dogs or cats. Everything is exotic. There is: a hutch full of wriggling biting ferrets which Brendan and Sean take out every Sunday after church to put down rabbit holes in the fields by the burn. A tame magpie called Maggie living in a big old wardrobe – if she likes you she lets you tickle her ear-tufts, if she doesn't she'll go for your eyes. Once she got out and dive-bombed Mrs Brown and her white hair was streaked red. That was the end of Maggie. 'She flew away,' said my mum, waving at the sky.

The Connors' shed has been extended into an aviary full of canaries which sing and sing till you think they'll burst. They hop spastically from perch to perch stopping every now and then to peck tiny perfectly round golden seeds. Danny shows me how to carefully blow the husks off the top so they can get to the good stuff. I want my own canary more than anything in the world and I usually get what I want. 'You'll spoil the laddie,' my dad warns, but he never says no. He bought me a rocking horse after he won on the Grand National. I plead and beg and they both make a show of saying no until one day Charlie appears in our living room in a golden cage all of his own. He's made of sunshine and songs. At night we put a tea towel over him so he goes to sleep.

Danny is a few months older than me and can do no wrong. He is my best friend in the whole world. His eyes are the green of the barley in the fields behind Granny Mac's house before they cut it and burn the stumps. He's magic with animals. He shows me not to be scared of the ferrets – to hold them tight to stop them biting. I let him play with my toys because his are all hand-me-downs and I don't mind if he bashes up my Tonka, I don't really bother with it anyway.

We've not started primary school yet. When we do we'll be separated. He'll go to St Theresa's, which is for the Catholics, and I'll go across the road to the 'non-denominational' Keir Hardie Memorial Primary with everybody else. My dad's Protestant and my mum's Catholic. I am neither. Or both. I can't work it out. For now we go to the same playschool every afternoon. In the Wendy house we act out bits from our favourite programmes – *Hart to Hart*, *CHiPs* and *Battlestar Galactica*. He never wants to be Mrs Hart but he does plant a kiss on my cheek at the end of every episode. I always start our games and I make sure it's just us in the Wendy house.

After playschool we all file out two-by-two holding hands to meet our mums at the gates where they wait smoking and gossiping. It's 3 p.m. but it's November so it's already dark and cold. There's Danny's mum but where's mine?

'Don't worry, son,' says Leena, seeing panic skitter across my face. 'Yer mammy's all right. She's in the hospital.'

Hospital! My lip starts to go. 'She's havin' the wean! Yer wee sister! Yer daddy's there an' all! She went in this mornin'.'

Leena puts her hand out and I notice her fingernails are chewed even shorter than my mum's. Danny takes one hand and I take the other and we walk back to 25 Ardgour Place. Wee sister, eh?

Danny and I sit end to end in our bath and we get away with splashing more than usual. Leena sits smoking on the toilet pan with the pink tasselled lid down flicking ash into the sink. Having only two weans to watch is a holiday for her – Gerry is next door with all the rest of hers. She jammies us up then makes us our tea . . . a treat I've dreamed of: Chicken and Mushroom Pot Noodle. We're even allowed to rip open the sachets of soya sauce and squirt them in ourselves. Just when we think it can't get any better we're told we're allowed to stay up because it's a Special Night.

Hart to Hart flies by and we all guess who did it. Then it's the News.

'Poor bastards,' says Leena, shaking her head. Danny doesn't flinch at the bad word and neither does she. 'Ah know they're English but . . .'

Gerry and Leena shout at each other all the time, we hear them through the walls, but 'bastard' has never been used in this house, not that I've heard. 'Let the poor bastards make a livin'. Under the ground, who wants to go under the ground every day? She'll no rest till they've no jobs, not wan. No wonder they're gonnae strike.'

Danny and I sip hot sweet tea and wish for the News to finish.

'Fuckin' witch! God forgive me, but ah hope she burns in hell, so she does.'

She doesn't look too scary, this blonde smiling woman they all hate. Whenever she comes on my dad turns it over: 'No coal, no steel, son. No coal, no steel.'

Next it's a programme I'm not even allowed to watch with my mum. It's eight o'clock – maybe even nine! The music for *Tales of the Unexpected* sounds like an ice-cream van slowed right down. It makes me feel funny. Skulls and puppets and playing cards birl round and round. It's like when my mum took me on the waltzers at the shows spinning round and round and the goldfish I won flew out the plastic bag of water and we had to watch it flipping slower and slower as we went round and round faster and faster. It stopped before we did. Once I sneaked out of bed and sat halfway down the stairs and watched this pro- gramme start through a crack in the living-room door before my dad caught me and carried me up. Now I am sitting in the living room watching it. If this is what happens when my mum has a baby I want a family as big as Danny's.

Flashes of lightning split the sky revealing a graveyard. The camera pans down across a headstone then goes below the ground through soil and tree roots then down into a coffin. Is there a body? A skeleton? Danny and I watch through our fingers pretending to be more scared than we are. Light flashes inside the coffin as a match is struck and I wonder why a dead person would smoke. It's a young blonde girl. Her face fills the telly as she realises where she is. The walls of the coffin are glass and she can see through them and she screams! And we scream too! And Leena decides 'Enough is enough' and leads us up to bed so we leave the girl in the glass coffin for ever.

I am in my *Battle of the Planets* pants and Danny is in his *Buck Rogers* pants. We're both in white vests, simmets, my dad calls them.

'Don't be telling yer mother I let yous watch that,' says Leena, tucking us in. She bribes us with a bag of salt and vinegar crisps from behind her back. 'Share nice,' she says, clicking off the light and heading back to the telly.

Danny pops the bag and we take turns tingling a crisp on our tongues. The Gas Scheme heating is on but I kid on I'm cold and snuggle in to Danny who puts his arm round me. Something hard pokes me. My pants start to feel tight so I slide them off, kicking them down my legs and over my toes. Danny does the same. The bed squeaks. I roll over to face him. This feels much warmer. We rub against each other, ignoring the crisp crumbs crunching under our legs. Danny rolls on top of me and we keep rubbing. This is new and good and we're out of breath but giggling. I pop another crisp in my mouth.

On snaps the light!

The squeaking and giggling have given us away. Leena starts to say something and I sit up knowing I've done something wrong. But what? I try saying sorry but I can't. I'm scared but it's not that stopping me. It's the crisp. The salt and vinegar crisp that is completely blocking my gullet. Jumping on the bed, totally pant-less, I tilt my head back and point at my mouth like a mad mime. My eyes are popping as I jump up and down.

Scared and trampled, Danny shouts, 'FUCK!'

Leena's face goes from angry to annoyed to afraid in a second as she pounces forward and picks me up. With one hand she crushes me to her chest – flat like my mum's – prising my mouth open with the other.

'Hold still,' she says.

I wriggle like a ferret. The crisp will not go down. I cannot cough it up. My eyes widen as she pushes her fingers in my mouth. 'CRK!' echoes in my head as she pokes through. Air whooshes into me. Carefully she lays me back on the bed.

Danny is already pretending he wasn't crying. Without being asked, we both put our pants back on (me in his, him in mine). Leena takes us back downstairs where she can watch us and the telly. The News is on again and it's the strikes and riots down south again. We take an armpit each.

'The pair of yous,' says Leena, looking down at us anxiously but not unkindly. 'Ah don't know. Yees are murder.'

'You mean moy-duh,' I say.

And we all laugh together like the Harts.

In the morning I wake late and Danny's already up cos the bed is empty. It really is a bit cold now so I jammy up and head downstairs. The clock says it's past lunchtime. Leena is drinking tea in the scullery with my dad who is usually sleeping or at work now.

'Where's ma mum?' I ask, looking round like she might be in one of the cupboards.

'Shhh, she's in bed, son,' says Leena, winking, and we wordlessly turn all of last night into a secret.

My dad picks me up and carries me over to the pram and we look down into it. There's a funny kind of basket in there and inside that there's a tiny bundle of pink wool with a face and masses of curly white-blonde hair.

'That's yer wee sister,' he says. 'Christine.'

'She's teenie!' I say, amazed by her smallness. And I love her.

2

'The future requires that industry adapt to produce goods that will sell in tomorrow's world. Older industries that can't change must be slimmed down . . .'
Margaret Thatcher, Airey Neave Memorial Lecture,
3 March 1980

F IRES BURN BENEATH MY feet. I've been warned that hell-red flames flicker and dance deep below the Bing and they'll eat up wee boys who don't do as they're told and stay away. I play here anyway, we all do. Wheezing from running I lie down on the smooth shiny coal dust that glitters impossibly black and press my face against the warmth I imagine down there. Certainly my face will be warm later when I'm trying to explain away my dirty clothes.

The Bing is a man-made wasteland of black slag heaps about two square miles. It takes me a good ten minutes to run here full sprint, the ground underfoot changing from the grey concrete slabs of Ardgour Place to football-scuffed playing fields to sparkling blackness. Teenie is a toddler now and follows me everywhere but I make sure the back gate's locked so she can't follow me down.

The Bing forms a barrier between Newarthill and the neighbouring village of New Stevenson where Granny and Granpa Barr live with their fat white cat Snowy. My mum says we don't visit them any more because when my dad wheeled the pram down to show me off Snowy fell asleep on my face and when my mum grabbed it by the tail and swung it over her head it was the cat they were upset about.

The Bing is mountains of sparkling black diamonds. No trees can take root on its loosely packed slopes which suddenly give way to cake-slice cliffs. Here and there a bright pink spire of rosebay willowherb flashes a warning. In the middle of it all there's a crater that's filled with rain over the years and become a great big pond burping with frogs.

Danny's never said anything about that night when Teenie was born and neither have I but I've not forgot. I wonder if he has. Every day we run down to the Bing as soon as our school bells ring at 3 p.m. We're still in our uniforms – mine the burgundy and sky-blue of Keir Hardie Memorial Primary School, his the dour brown of St Theresa's Primary School. In summer the sun never really sets here – you're further north than you think. There's always a patch of snow-wash denim blue in the indigo of the night. We know the Soviets are pointing nuclear missiles at us because Glasgow, as Mr Baker points out on the multicoloured globe one day, is on the same latitude as Moscow. The bell rings and we all imagine it's the two-minute warning. What will we do? Maggie's parked her nuclear submarines in a loch somewhere and there's more marches on the News, angry women chained to fences. Will she have time to fire back? It doesn't matter anyway. It's the Argies, not the Russians we're fighting

Last week the whole school, except Primary One, had an emergency assembly and Miss Carey the headmistress told us calmly that we were at war with Argentina and even I didn't know where it was until she showed us on the globe. The teachers standing behind her looked bored.

I hope the war doesn't come here because I don't want my dad to have to be a soldier. We watch the *BBC News at One* and it's all Union Jacks and boats and planes. Two teachers point and laugh when they show Maggie wearing a headscarf driving a tank but I think she looks good, brave, glamorous even. She'll show them!

Days last for ever. There are no adults to stop us doing whatever we want – so long as we're back home for our tea they're not worried. Me and Danny and his gang spend whole summers at the Bing. What do we do? How do we fill all that time? We make our own fun!

For starters, we play frog tennis. This is exactly what it sounds like . . . you kick your Adidas Gazelles off, roll your trouser legs up and squelch into the slippery slimy edges of the water, trying not to make a face as the cold mud pushes between your toes because you'll get called a poof if you do. You stand very still till the beautiful golden-eyed frogs forget you're there and one swims close enough to catch. The frog is the ball. Its arms and legs splay as you throw it in the air, the sun shining through its webbed feet, before you smash it with your bat. What's left arcs towards your opponent who leaps like he's on Centre Court. The first time I hit a frog hard enough for it not just to die but explode in death, covering me in guts and gore and guilt, is the last time I play that game. You didn't really understand, I tell myself. I feel ashamed. The other boys play round after round, even Danny.

Danny's friends don't like me like he does, they don't really like me at all – they only put up with me because of him. I'm acceptable by association. I know that but I'm not bothered enough to make other friends. They all think they know something about me but they'd never suspect Danny. He's the golden-haired hero boy who can run and jump and punch all at once like the Karate Kid. He always defends me and only ever calls me 'Barr' to toughen me up. As usual, everybody copies him. I have to run faster, jump higher and punch harder to prove I'm one of them – and I desperately want to be one of them – and when I fall, as I usually do, this only confirms their suspicions and makes them hate me more. I am too different – too tall, my school trousers are sneaking so far up my shins my new nickname is 'Half-mast'. I'm too skinny, too clever . . . too Protestant. 'Proddy Dogs eat the frogs on a Sunday morning,' they all sing to a cheery tune.

One Saturday they're cheering cos Celtic has won, the team of all Catholics in the West of Scotland, the Pope's own players. They wave the green, white and gold of the Irish flag. They've beaten Rangers, the team that's supposed to be mine because I might as well be a Proddy: Rangers, the red, white and blue of the Union Jack – the Queen's own boys. Some Catholics paint gold-and-white stripes on their lawn to make the Irish flag. Proddies retaliate by painting the kerbs red, white and blue.

Danny jumps about chanting 'FTQ! FUCK THE QUEEN! FTQ! FUCK THE QUEEN!'

I hate feeling left out but don't know the words to join in. My mum told me to say 'I support my legs and my legs support me' when asked what team I support. This lameness guarantees you'll get beaten up so I usually try one or the other depending if the boys asking look Catholic or not. So what are Proddy Dogs supposed to bark?

'FTP!' I burst, remembering to punch the air. 'Fuck the Pope!'

Sudden and total silence. Then, they're on me.

Kicking and punching from all directions and I really do see Scooby-Doo stars. Instinctively I roll into a ball, making myself as small a target as possible, choking on the coal dust sucking into my asthmatic lungs. I squeeze my eyelids closed and will them to get bored and stop. They're always calling me 'Damien Omen' – Danny says he's seen a pirate video – so maybe I've got secret powers. They're not working now. When my nose bursts Danny calls them off. It reminds me of when Granny Mac pulled three dogs off this really harassed-looking dog in the park one day, a finger raised warning me not to ask what they were all doing.

Danny looks me over in a glance only I see. Punishment for your sins – that's the Catholic way. He helps me to my feet then kicks them straight out from under me and I fall to my knees winded. That hurts more than anything.

The hills of the Bing were bulldozed into being by the big yellow JCB diggers that came for the last of the coal before I was born. There's still a wee bit of coal. When the News is full of strikes and the coal man stops coming round with his big lorry some older boys burrow into the Bing with the shovels for cleaning ashes out the fireplace. They go round the doors of the Coal Scheme selling what they dig up. More than one boy dies, suffocating in a collapsed tunnel. Maybe they turn to coal. Sometimes a whole field falls back into the ground, leaving a perfect circle like a hot mug on a table. The Bing has one really scary cliff – a sheer drop of about thirty feet we've dared each other to jump off for years. Nobody ever has. Not even Danny. We imagine doing wheelies off it.

Only one of us has a BMX – me, an eighth birthday present from my dad. I love riding it but I'm too scared to be a bandit like the ones on Saturday *Swap Shop*. I'm happy to let everybody else do stunts. They like me more then.

The boy who pulls the biggest wheelies and hates me the most pins my hands behind my back. Paddy's lips are jagged like they were cut out of his face with the pinking shears you need to ask the teacher's permission to use. He nods towards the cliff edge. My heart falls.

'You or yer bike. Pick wan.'

If my BMX is mangled I might as well be dead because my dad will kill me even though he's never actually hit me for anything. I've never been hit even when I deserved it. Last summer he left his shed unlocked and not thinking it was a funny place to find a bottle of Barr's Cola and not wondering why it didn't fizz when I managed to open it and not wondering why it smelled, I took a big gulp. It was creosote. Burning, spewing up my stomach and trying to run away because I didn't want to get in trouble, flashing blue lights, stomach pump, weeks of sympathy and no punishment. If Paddy makes me jump I'll end up one of those pissy-smelling kids in a wheelchair that everybody hates. On the upside, I'll get loads of sympathy and I'll never have to do gym again.

I start crying, thinking maybe they'll find this so embarrassing they'll stop. WRONG! They all laugh.

'Aww, he's greeting,' laughs Paddy, rubbing his eyes. 'Want yer mammy?'

Danny grips my hands behind my back less tightly but not so's anybody can see. His hard body is pressing against mine and he breathes in to speak, to set me free.

'How about this, boys, how about we make him jump?'

22

JUMP?! Some pal! I can't believe this – my best pal in the whole world is offering me up to them. I feel like Aslan on the stone table.

'Let's make it more interestin',' he says and goes over to them and whispers.

For a second I'm free so I run. I run and I run and I run until Paddy tackles me to the ground and drags me back kicking and screaming and coughing up enough coal for a fire. Danny leads a bunch of them back towards the houses where our mothers sit in ignorance.

They're away for ever but probably only half an hour. I chat with the others like nothing's happened. Paddy ignores me. Without a leader there's no one to be cruel in front of but we all know they can't let me go. In the distance the others return carrying something on their shoulders.

It's a coffin.

I start struggling. Fuck, they're going to bury me alive. It's *Tales of the Unexpected* only nobody's going to rescue me just before the air runs out. I'm going to be buried in the black ground for ever with those other boys. My bones will turn to coal. Oh God, oh God . . . they're getting closer. I try shaking them off but they're stuck. The coffin comes closer and I can see it properly. It's not a coffin. It's, it's a great big wardrobe, the dark old-fashioned ones that are getting chucked out as MDF gets trendy up here. My mum's thrilled with her newly fitted bedroom suite. This must be the wardrobe that Maggie the Magpie lived in.

Danny winks at me. What? What joke am I missing? This isn't funny. I think about shitting myself to gross them out so much they'll have to let me go but I'd never live it down so I watch them walk the wardrobe to the edge of the cliff, inching forward corner-to-corner cos the slag heaps are crumbly and they don't want to fall before I do. It stands with its back to the drop. Then, like hotel bellboys in the black-and-white films Granny Mac loves, they swing the door open and invite me to step in. As if I have a choice.

An exploding wardrobe is great fun to watch but it's even better knowing a boy is inside. I have to admit that – I'd played frog tennis.

Danny smiles as he gently closes the door on me and I realise this is an act of love. The wardrobe will break my fall. Paddy would have made me jump without it. Inside smells of mothballs and I think of Narnia, sure I won't find it in this wardrobe, when something soft brushes my face. Dangling on the clothes rail is a mess of cloth – sheets, maybe, or curtains. They stink of old people but I wrap them round me. Danny did this. '10, 9, 8, 7, 6 . . .' They count down outside, muffled by the door. '5, 4, 3, 2 . . . ONE!'

I feel them all round me pushing. For a second nothing happens. Then there is only air above and below. We don't spin or topple, the wardrobe and me. In total darkness we drop like a stone . . . straight down for what seems like for ever and I brace myself, careful not to put my tongue between my teeth because I remember Mr Baker telling us not to in gym. Cool calm floods my veins like the antifreeze in my dad's Escort. I take deep breaths and think of my mum and my wee sister and my dad and hope they all cry for me. I hold the rail above me like the yuppies on London trains on the News and surely I must hit the ground soon and right then a light so bright bursts in as the wardrobe explodes around me.

It is a million matchsticks.

I'm in one piece.

I'm not dead. I've survived. I'm a hero! They lift me on to Danny's shoulders and everybody's whooping and singing and dancing around us high on destruction. I'm still not dead. Not just *not dead* but fucking brilliant. I feel amazing! I AM POPULAR! I've not broken a single bone, not even got a small cut on my cheek to show for it. I'm shaking so much I fall off Danny's shoulders and they crowd round me again only now they're slapping me on the back chanting 'Barr! Barr! Barr!' Everybody except Paddy. He stands apart and stares at me like he'll never blink again and I don't look back because I don't want to see what he sees.

I run home more alive than I've ever been and burst through the back gate, reaching the steps before it's even clicked closed. On the top step I hear shouting and inside the house is suitcases and tears. My mum's trying to pull the rings from her fingers but she can't get them off and my dad's saying she's brought it all on herself. Teenie is three already but can't find the words to make them stop so she's just bawling and I run to her and cuddle her and tell her it'll all be OK.

'Ah'm leavin' and ah'm taking them wae me!' shouts my mum and I think she means her rings then I see she means us. 'C'mon, Damian!' she shouts, grabbing at my hand.

She never shouts and she never ever shouts at me. There's never been a row in this house, not that I've heard. I throw her hand down and run past her upstairs and she shouts, 'Damian Leighton Barr!' I keep trying to think what I've done wrong and run into their room, which I'm not allowed in, heading straight for the fitted wardrobe my mum begged for.

I've only just got behind her best coat and the rabbit fur's tickling my nose as I wheeze in and out when the floorboards creak their special Dad creak. Downstairs the back door slams.

'Damian, son,' he says from outside the wardrobe. I say nothing and try to breathe as quietly as I can. 'Damian, son,' he repeats right outside the door.

We both know where I am and we both know he won't open the door. Slowly I push the coat out the way and the MDF sags under my feet as I reach for the door. Light floods in and I blink at my dad sitting on the already empty bed.

I glance at the bedroom door.

'They're away already,' he says and I start towards it but he catches my trouser loop with one finger and I run in the air like Roadrunner off a cliff. 'They're only away tae yer Granny Mac's,' he says but I don't believe him. 'They'll be back.' He looks away and I don't think he believes himself either.

I don't understand any of this. My dad sits me on his knee and we both sit staring into the wardrobe through the open door.

'Yer mammy,' he starts. 'She's. Ah. We. Ah.'

I turn round to cuddle him and my arms still don't go all the way round. 'Ah'm not going anywhere, Daddy,' I say, angry at my mum and Teenie for leaving us and planning a proper tantrum for when they get back even though I'm a bit old for that at eight.

Our tea that night is a casserole delivered over the back fence by Leena. She smiles at me but she's got nothing but dirty looks for my dad, who mumbles thanks and takes the dish back himself, the first time I've ever seen him wash up. I listen at the fence.

'Glenn Barr, you've only yersel tae blame,' says Leena before Gerry tells her to can it because it's none of her business.

'She's made her bed,' says my dad.

Who has? What bed?

'And do you blame her? She lost that wee lassie and where've you been?' shouts Leena. 'It wisnae the Craig that needed ye!'

Gerry says, 'enough's enough,' and their gate clicks as my dad comes back.

Gerry and Leena keep arguing and I run upstairs to brush my teeth as if my mum was here to check. Doors are slamming over and over as I fall asleep. A massive smash in the night and I sit up. Can I hear birds singing? Back to sleep. When I get up my dad's sleeping next to me, a giant teddy in Y-fronts. His eyes are closed but I know they're the blue of my favourite marble, the one I won't play with in case I lose it. He's like Mr Hart only he doesn't really talk. 'Yer daddy's a man of few words,' says my mum, 'that's how come he's got me.' I climb over him and go downstairs to make his breakfast as a surprise.

In the scullery I stand on the bunker to get to the cupboard where the tea bags live. I look out the scullery window. A miracle. All the Browns' roses have come out overnight. It's October. I rub the sleep from my eyes with one hand and hold on to the cupboard door with the other so I don't fall. I squint through the net curtains that my mum's always bleaching whiter than white. Some of the roses are yellow but some look red and I don't remember any red ones and it must be really windy outside because they look like they're moving. Charlie is flapping madly in his cage in the living room. My dad appears behind me and lifts me off the bunker folding my scream into his chest as I realise that the flowers have feathers.

3

'It was a lovely morning. We have not had many lovely days. And the sun was just coming through the stained-glass windows and falling on some flowers right across the church and it just occurred to me that this was the day I was meant not to see.'

Margaret Thatcher, interview for Channel 4,
15 October 1984

M Y MUM, MY WEE sister and me are now living with Logan in Flat 1, 1 Magdalene Drive, Carfin. Everything is unpacked but I still don't really believe I'll have to stay here with this red-faced man who makes the air shake. It's a mistake – we'll move back in with my dad any day now. It's nearly Christmas already and we can't have Christmas without him. I'm now in Primary Four and Teenie is starting playschool.

Primary Four is heady with hyacinths. Because of them I've sneezed about a hundred times and both my sleeves are wet with watery snot. I'm worried the snot will ruin the effect of my carefully ironed-on transfers of roses which came with a *Woman's Own* I snaffled from my auntie Louisa. The roses are biro blue and totally unnatural but I love them.

At the start of term each of the twenty-six members of Primary Four planted a papery bulb in an individual terracotta-coloured plastic pot labelled with their name. It's now December and the unpromising bulbs are blooming. Every. Single. One. For reasons only he knows, Mr Baker has lined them all up on the boiling cast-iron radiators. It's nearly playtime and the flowers, like the pupils, are drooping. We all need watering.

We're doing decimals and they're so boring I want to die. They seem pointless. The blackboard has been rolled round from the bit with lines on, which promises letters and words, to the bit with squares on, which threatens numbers and sums. The week we went from familiar fractions to decimals I was off with an asthma attack. Everybody else is thrilled with a sneeze but I would do anything to stay in school, not to be in that flat with that man. If I could I'd sleep on the narrow single bed in the school clinic with clean white sheets and comfortingly tight hospital corners. I'd lie there with my arms by my sides reading *Little Women* again. I wouldn't be any trouble.

For the first time ever I don't understand what Mr Baker is blethering about and I won't ask because everybody in the class will look at me and laugh which isn't unusual but I always know everything and won't admit I can't do decimals. I'm used to feeling embarrassed about being the tallest and the skinniest and my 'broken home' but I'm not used to feeling stupid so I stay quiet.

Mr Baker has a black moustache which grows out of his nose. Maybe it's all just his nose hair and not an actual moustache made of face hair like my dad's. When he throws his head back to make a point I see right up his nostrils. His specs grip his nose trying hard to hold on. They have silver metal legs and milk-bottle lenses so thick they make his eyes look small and slightly surprised. Bushy black eyebrows sprout over the top.

The big radiators round the edge of the class are pumping out so much heat I can actually see it. School is always warmer than home so I am not complaining. I sneak a peek at my Timex. It's 10.30 a.m. Soon the playtime bell will ring. We hear it extra loud in Primary Four because we're right at the end of the corridor where the red bell clangs high on the wall. I think we get more playtime than other classes because we hear it first. I'd rather we didn't.

Our desks are arranged in a horseshoe shape, 'So I can see everybody and everybody can see everybody else,' said Mr Baker when he made us move them on the first day of Primary Four. There's no longer a front of the class for me to sit at. To my right is the classroom door. To my left is Amanda Ferguson. She outlines all her drawings in black felt tip so they look like comics. Her dad deals off the back of a lorry so she's always got great stuff but sometimes it's dodgy. Instead of *PUMA* her schoolbag says *POMO* which sounds like 'homo' and we all laugh but don't really know why. It's a word we've heard the Primary Sevens use. She's the first girl in our class to boast a full spiral perm in tribute to Kylie off *Neighbours* and it's always crispy with mousse. I reach out to touch it and she slaps my hand away. The movement catches Mr Baker's eye even though he is busy with some 0.5 something and he works himself up to the rare pleasure of shouting at me. I lower my eyes and place my hands flat down in front of me and the brown wood-effect Formica desk feels cool against my instantly sweaty palms. I feel my face go red. I breathe in and out so slowly my chest doesn't rise or fall. I am learning how to make angry men calm down. Mr Baker turns back to his blackboard.

Mr Baker's chalk snaps just before his patience and he sends Pete Downie to the supply cupboard that sits behind foldaway doors in a corner of the classroom. If he's in a right rage Mr Baker will actually grab you by the scruff of your neck and throw you in it. Pete has been hurled in loads of times and locked in once or twice. Because his head is oddly oval his nickname is 'Egg'. He's pure cheek. Egg drags his feet over to the cupboard then speeds up like Benny Hill when Mr Baker shouts. He scurries back with the chalk and Mr Baker cuffs his ear. If you're a chatterbox like me you get your mouth taped up with Sellotape that tastes like flypaper smells. Eventually it steams up and peels off as you huff and puff through your nostrils.

10.50 a.m and Mr Baker is giving up on decimals about an hour after I did. He walks to his desk at the front of the class and picks up the book he's been reading aloud to us. When he reads his voice is deeper and more regular than when he shouts. It's the only time he's really calm and it's the only time we really listen to him. *The Witches* is my favourite Roald Dahl book ever – way better than *Fantastic Mr Fox* or *Danny, the Champion of the World* (although I love Danny's dad). The witches are terrifying because they look like nice ladies who might take you in if you lost your way and offer to make you tea and toast while your mum comes to fetch you. Only the tea will turn you into a frog or worse. While Mr Baker reads on I try to remember what it's like to want to go home. I try to remember what it's like to be lost and want to be found.

He looks at his watch because he's allowed to. Even through his spider-leg arm hairs I can see it's 10.55 a.m. He should be sending the milk monitor out to fetch the crate.

School milk is not like home milk or milk in adverts. For starters it comes in special triangular cardboard cartons with a tiny silver foil dot that you pierce with a red straw so thin you've got to suck your cheeks right in to get it going. They're piled up in sour sick-smelling 50p-shaped crates that magically appear outside the classroom during morning lessons. You can spray someone with the milk if you squeeze the carton hard enough or stab them with the straw if you jab it fast and hard just once holding the straw near the sharp end (any more or from the other end and it snaps). School milk is not rich and cold and creamy. It is watery and slightly grey and too warm. But you have to drink your milk. The older I get the quicker I drain my carton. At the end of the day spare milks, undrunk by absent pupils, are given out as prizes for answering general knowledge questions fired out by Mr Baker. I usually win extra milk this way. Sometimes I take that milk home for my mum's tea.

This week Amanda Ferguson is our milk monitor and she's shifting in her seat next to me, one leg out from under the desk ready to dash to the door on Mr Baker's command, but he keeps on reading. This is her moment. All the witches are at a conference and they're planning something really big, something super evil. Something is about to happen.

Amanda Ferguson can't sit still any more. 'Mr Baker, sir, the milk!' she says as if there is a tidal wave of milk that will drown us all if we don't do something NOW! 'The milk!' she repeats, sweeping a crispy curl from her face as he slowly places the book down open at the page where she stopped him.

Twenty-five heads turn as one and stare at Amanda Ferguson, who will surely be chucked in the stationery cupboard for shouting out in class and interrupting Mr Baker's reading. She might even get her big pink mouth taped up.

'Thank you, Amanda,' he says, almost politely.

Twenty-five mouths breathe out – simultaneously relieved that a popular pupil is not getting shouted at but also slightly disappointed.

'There will be no more milk –'

'But –' interrupts Amanda.

'But nothing, Amanda! There's milk today but soon there won't be any for the same reason you've had no new jotters. For the same reason the staff have gone on strike.'

We've definitely not had fresh jotters this term. We're reusing the ones we filled up – rubbing out all the work takes ages and sometimes the paper rips. You've got to blow away all the dirty grey bits. They're like sunburnt skin you've peeled off and rolled between your fingers, only there's nothing fresh or new below. Everybody but me has novelty rubbers – strawberry-shaped and scented or with *Greetings from Lanzarote* printed on. If you squint hard you can see the ghosts of old words peeking through. Will I remember what I've rubbed out?

'The Prime Minster of England,' starts Mr Baker, and I don't like to point out that Margaret Hilda Thatcher is the Prime Minister of Great Britain and that Scotland is a part of Great Britain and has been since the Act of Union 1707. Nobody likes a know-it-all. 'She's stopped free milk in schools down there already and now she's trying to stop it up here as well and if she does we won't be needing any milk monitors any more.'

Amanda Ferguson might lose her job. We all might. Her mouth forms a perfect *O*. I want to draw a black line around it.

'If we have time we'll return to *The Witches* at the end of the day,' says Mr Baker as the playtime bell rings and one of the hyacinths finally topples over.

After the home-time bell that day I wait at the zebra crossing with the lollipop lady, who looks at me like I'm going the wrong way. Keir Hardie sits on top of a steep brae and it's icy all winter but I'm not interested in sledging down with the boys from my class, I just want to get back home. Side-stepping the treacherous tarmac I carefully crunch down the hill on the frosty grass. Boys shoot past me on 'borrowed' bin-lids like X-Wing Fighters escaping the exploding Death Star before finally coming to rest in slushy puddles by the house my mum now calls 'yer dad's'.

I go in the back gate and turn the door handle. It's locked. It's never locked. There's no smell of dinner cooking, no steam on the window from tatties boiling to mush because my mum can't cook, no matter how hard she tries. I knock with my mittened hand but it's muffled so I unsnuggle my fingers and wish my mum would get that I'm grown up enough for gloves. The red paint on the back door of 25 Ardgour Place seems to say stop but I knock again anyway. I start banging. It's colder and harder than ice against my knuckles. Still no answer. I go round the front and peek through the letterbox, a strange new view. My dad's not there but he'll be home soon and maybe then he can explain why I've got to walk half a mile back to Carfin and the strange flat crowded without him when I could just stay here.

I sit on the freezing-cold step – the middle step of three – and note it's dirty beneath the snow. There's a footprint I don't recognise, like someone stamped the bottom of a can in the snow and then, a few inches behind, a pencil. Was it some weird animal? It's not the Browns' big St Bernard, he's always got a bucket on his head because his droopy red-rimmed eyes get infected. I look round for stray Thundercats. All I see is windows glowing warm and flashes of Gordon the Gopher causing chaos in the BBC's Broom Cupboard. I hate that Gopher. Soon *Dungeons and Dragons* will be on with those all-American kids fighting the winged fanged lisping Venger to get back home. Or maybe it'll be *Ulysses 31*: Uly-see-eee-es, Uly-see-eee-es, falling through the galaxies, could not find his dest-in-y!

What light there was has drained away and it's now so dark my dad almost lands on me as he takes the steps in one leap.

'For fuck's sake, Damian!' He never swears. Then, worried: 'What are ye doin' here? Yer freezin'!' He grabs my hands, rubs them, as if I could choose to be warmer. He clasps both my hands in one of his and hoists me up while unlocking the door with the other. 'Come away in,' he says, as if I need inviting into my own house. He's black as usual from his shift at the Craig, blacker in the snow.

In our scullery again I start taking off my coat.

'Damian, son, what are ye doin'?'

Without answering I walk to the under-stairs cupboard and hang up my coat instead of throwing it over a chair. I smile up at my dad hoping for approval for doing something right without having to be asked. He looks sad. What have I done? How can I make it better? He stands in his overalls the colour of the night gathering its thoughts outside the window then slowly sinks to his knees on the terracotta-effect lino my mum loves. I step forward to catch him knowing I can't and he pulls me in, crushing me to his chest till I've no air left and can't breathe in again but don't care. My school shirt will be filthy, I think, sucking in the smell of him I didn't know I'd missed — coal and warmth and something sparkling like quartz.

I only realise he's crying when tears roll past my collar down my neck. 'Oh son,' he says over and over. 'Oh son.'

I can't cry. I want to but I'm more scared than sad because I've not seen my dad cry before.

He holds me at arm's length with his hands weighing on my shoulders and looks at me as if seeing me for the first time. For once we're the same height. His sooty face is streaked with white like reverse mascara tears.

'This isnae yer home any more, son.'

I stare dumbly.

He sounds his next words carefully. 'You don't live here any more.'

I try to get away because if I can just get to my room I can slide under my bed and hide and everything will be all right so I wriggle and jump and shout 'NO!' and eventually he lets me go. I leap the stairs in twos and swing into my room on the door handle, slamming it behind me.

Cowboys and Indians are still yee-hawing and wa-wa-wa-wahing across the walls and Paddington Bear still has his hand in the marmalade pot on the curtains. But there's no bed. I stand staring at the empty bed-shaped space where I've always slept and ignore the door opening behind me. I jump when I feel my dad's hands on my shoulders. *Then* I cry. Scalding childish tears, worse than my wee sister at her worst, they run into the snotters streaming from my nose now I've come in from the cold.

'We better get ye home to yer mum,' says my dad, but he doesn't move and neither do I.

'But this is my home!'

'No, it's not. Not any more. C'mon, son, stop yer greetin'.'

I'm trying to stop, to be brave. I'm making that weird panicky h–hu–huh noise breathing in stops and starts, my chin tipping up. Tears dry tight on my hot face. My dad is pulling me into my Paddington duffel coat. My arms are limp. I couldn't help even if I wanted to.

'C'mon, Damian,' he pleads. 'Help me out here, son.'

I turn round and find I can pull my coat on after all. He walks downstairs ahead of me and into the scullery where my mittens wait on the floor. I pull my blue wellies back on while my dad makes a phone call, his fingers barely fitting in the dial. I don't recognise the number.

'The laddie disnae know if he's comin' or gawn,' he says, turning away, pushing his big rumbling voice into the white plastic handset. I imagine his breath catching in the tiny holes in the receiver and I want to lick it. A minute later he bangs it down, picks his car keys up and opens the back door.

I just stand there. I can't leave, I won't leave. So he carries me out to our car, a red Ford Escort with black spoiler, even though I am eight and embarrassed to be carried. Then, instead of putting me in the back, he sits me in the front and shows me how to put the seatbelt on. I've been promoted.

'You're the man of the house now,' he says. 'Not long and you'll have yer own motor.'

We drive up the hill past Keir Hardie Memorial Primary School and on to Carfin arriving five cruelly fast minutes later.

My mum is standing outside, arms crossed, and I worry she's not got a coat on. The scullery window blazes with cold fluorescent light and in it Logan is silhouetted. When I see him I try to get back in the car but my dad's undone my seat-belt and my mum is reaching out for me. Danny did get *The Omen* and we watched it and it's like that bit where they try to take Damien to church. I'm shouting 'NO' and grabbing at the door. My dad keeps both hands on the steering wheel staring straight ahead, no blinking. His knuckles are white underneath the dirt from work.

My mum starts crying. 'Why? Why did ye go there? Ye know ye live here now, I was worried sick, yer wee sister's been cryin', don't you dare do that again.' Out it all tumbles.

My dad leans over the now empty passenger seat, pulling the door closed with his left hand before looking over his shoulder and reversing away. I feel like I'll never see him again. I feel like I'm leaving myself, leaving the world. He doesn't look back or pip his horn as he speeds up. My mum kneels in the snow pressing me into her non-existent boobs and sobs. I can't cry any more. Over her I see Logan and his shadowed shoulders are bobbing. He's chuckling.

From then on I do as I'm told and don't go home – as I still think of it – until custody is sorted. I watch *Kramer vs. Kramer* with my mum one Sunday and we're both crying and she says she'd never give us up and anyway the courts never give men custody. My dad gets us every second weekend. Did he not want us more?

Every day I drag my feet, with the laces tucked down the sides of the shoes because I won't admit I still can't tie them, back to the flat. Every day I dread it – fear the bell at three o'clock. I walk the half-mile back to Carfin measuring each kerbstone in six baby-steps and I take one step back for every six forward. This way I make a fifteen-minute journey last forty-five minutes.

The mood in the flat gets heavier with my mum. She looked normal when we moved in but now she looks like she's about to pop again. She actually waddles in a big navy-blue maternity dress with a ridiculous white bow around her belly. She jokes that she looks like Demis Roussos in his kaftan and we used to dance to his records when my dad was at the Craig. Granny Mac and Auntie Louisa used to bring Tea Cakes at least twice a week but they hardly ever visit us in Carfin. As my mum gets bigger they finally appear, huffing and fussing, following her round with a wee red cushion for her back. Auntie Louisa smiles small smiles, saying things like, 'Not long till yer better, hen.' Granny Mac doesn't take her coat off and loudly says nothing while bleaching every surface in sight. She hangs a cross over my mum's bed.

Months go by and my Mum balloons. We have two Christmases – one at my dad's and one at my mum's – and maybe divorce isn't all bad. One day in February I get home from school as late as possible, as usual. It's already pitch black. I look up at the scullery window expecting my mum smiling down and instead there's Logan. I freeze. Where is she? I think about turning round and running away but he's seen me now and where would I go? I'd only have to come back. So I take the five steps slowly, one by one, and tiptoe along the communal hallway which always smells of wet dog and bleach and walk into Flat 1, 1 Magdalene Drive.

Logan stands in the scullery. He is smiling. I have never seen a smile stay on his face and it makes me feel funny behind my knees. I try smiling back but can't and turn to scuttle to my room but he grabs my schoolbag, jerking me back so I swing round to face him.

'Whoa there, Pussy Willow.' He always calls me this when my mum's not there.

That or 'Jessy' or 'Princess' or 'Bent Shot'. He knows I'm different and sets about making me hate myself before I know myself. He hates me. I feel it hot on my face like the anticipation of a slap. He doesn't bother with Teenie, doesn't seem to notice her.

Logan is a plumber for British Gas. 'Fuckin' Tories,' he says when the adverts come on the telly. 'Fuckin' Maggie. Shares? Share this, Sid!' He sticks two fingers up.

His blue work satchel is full of hefty wrenches and foul-smelling glues. He works his own hours which means I never know if he's in or out. He enjoys this. My dad works regular shifts at the Craig – I see them in the sky and know he'll be home not long after he's finished pouring out tons of liquid steel turning it all the reds and oranges. My dad makes the sun set twice every night and when I see it I know he's there. The only time I know for sure that Logan will be out is 11 a.m. till 4 p.m. every Sunday when he goes to his mother's to clean out his pigeons and coo at them with a tenderness you can't imagine. Only then can I breathe out and that's when I take my bath. His pigeon dookit fills the back garden of his mother's terraced house in New Stevenson – right across the road from Granny Barr. Him and my dad were boys together.

'Right, Princess, time for yer tea,' he says, spinning me round the scullery like in a game of blind man's bluff.

I don't wait to be told twice but work up the courage to ask where my mum is.

Logan doesn't like questions. 'She's at the hospital and she'll be back the morra wi yer wee brother.' So this bump is a boy. What if it's like him? 'Don't look so delighted,' he says, smile gone. 'Things are gonnae change round here,' he says, turning to the cooker he fitted that I've never seen him use.

He picks up a bowl from the bunker and ladles out what looks like pea and ham soup. He hands me a brimming bowl which is unusual because if ever mum pops out and he has to feed us we get half-portions and I get called 'Oliver' for asking for more, which he never gives me. The soup is too hot and burns my lips but I don't complain because I want to get away to my bedroom and my books.

He stands smiling, watching me eat. 'Yer wee sister's in bed awready,' he says, and I think of Teenie cuddled up with the doll she ignores during the day cos she hates people thinking she's girly. She'd rather have a football. Logan encourages her to support Rangers and says she's more of a man than me. 'Straight tae sleep after yer homework – nae readin' for you the night.'

I focus on the pattern on the bowl, big red roses like the ones climbing round my bedroom window at my dad's. I eat as quickly as I can without being accused of rushing and rest my spoon quietly on the bowl when I'm done because Logan hates clanking.

'Please can I go and do my homework now?' I ask.

'Please can I go and do my homework now?' he sing-songs straight back in a high-girly parody, waving the ladle like a fairy wand. 'Away ye go,' he says, lowering his voice and leaning down so I can feel his hot beery breath on my face. 'BOO!' and I bolt into my room and close the door, careful not to slam it.

All I can think is: I am alone here with him. I have dreaded this ever since we moved here. My wee sister is sleeping in her room. My mum is in hospital giving birth to my brother. I struggle with my long division picturing Logan in the living room just across the hallway. There's no mum here. I catch bits of a one-sided conversation. He's on the phone, which we use so rarely I sometimes forgot we've got one. I could call my dad but I don't know his new number. It's been changed. Logan sounds happy and I hear laughing, real laughter, and then the 'PSSHT' of another can of Tennent's. He doesn't usually drink.

I finish the last sum and get into my Superman jammies. My mum's not here to light the fire in my room – the Carfin flats don't have central heating. From the window over my bed a dirty orange streetlight glows through the thin, porridge-coloured curtains then a bigger brighter cleaner light as my dad empties the furnaces. I roll on my side, pulling my knees up to my chest, and cuddle myself. I hope Teenie's warmer than me. The light fades and I do times tables in my head until sleep happens.

I am awake.

Flat on my back gagging and gasping. I lean my head over the side of the bed and hot wet chunks spray on the carpet so hard they bounce back flecking my face. Panicking, I clamp my hand over my mouth to stop whatever it is from coming up but it flies through my fingers and goes up my sleeves. My favourite jammies ruined, think of the trouble I'll be in. I jump out of bed straight into the hot mess slipping and sliding as I run for the light. Flicking it on I see brown and green lumps everywhere steaming like dog shit in the cold air. I open my bedroom door and stagger to the bathroom but fall on my knees in the hallway. Terrified by the force of the vomit spraying out of me I close my streaming eyes and pray for it to stop. I'm not even gagging, it just keeps coming. Gasping for air on all fours I only gulp lumps down. Where's my mum? Hospital? Somehow Teenie stays asleep.

Logan comes to my rescue.

Grabbing me by the scruff of my neck he pulls me up into the air bursting the top button off my pyjama jacket. For a second I fly like Superman.

'Wit the fuck?' Logan shakes me like a piggybank. 'Wit the fuck?!' He's shouting now and staring at his feet, disgusted at what he's stood in. 'Bastard!' he shouts, shaking me so hard my eyes rattle in my head. 'Clean this fuckin' mess up!' He shakes me even harder and I can't stop the lumps rising and as I spew at him he drops me in the cooling mess that now has a school-custard skin. 'Ten minutes, clean it up,' he says. 'Wi yer fuckin' hands.' And he goes into the bathroom and closes the door and I hear the bath start running.

With my hands? I look down at them. Then what? Put it where? He's in the bathroom so I can't flush it and I can't trail it through the living room to the scullery bin. Time is running out. I will Teenie's door to stay closed. She can't see this. I feel empty now but the smell and the taste in my mouth make me gag. All I can think to do is what I do. I start scooping with my hands and filling my pockets. I retch as my trouser pockets brim and bulge. My pyjama jacket is covered anyway so I pull it off and make a sort of bag, tying the sleeves together like Dick Whittington did when he left for London. This works and I've almost filled it when the bathroom door opens.

'Leave it,' commands Logan, steam curling round him.

I put it down, noting proudly that it does not leak.

'Strip,' he says.

I peel the clammy trousers off, leg by leg, and step out of them. I'm covered in my own sick and freezing.

'In,' he says, pointing at the steaming bath, white cast-iron like all the baths in all the flats in Magdalene Drive but boxed in with plywood, not claw-footed like in the Flake advert. 'In,' he repeats, grabbing one of my arms, dangling me up over the edge before dropping me.

It's boiling and I leap right up gasping but he pushes me back. He sits on the toilet lid staring at me. I look down at myself. My skin is now as red as his face. I see my bald willy which refuses to catch up with the other boys. He catches me looking and laughs.

'Wash,' he says quietly, rhyming it harshly with 'ash'. He's no longer shouting.

I stare at him and try standing up again. I jump up, sloshing water over the sides. Logan stays sitting but lowers his eyes slowly and I find myself sitting down again, under a spell.

Chunks float in an oily scum and the steam carries their stench. I start focusing on details, noticing lumps of carrot and wondering why there's always carrot in sick, then realise there must have been some in the soup. The soup. The soup he made for me but did not eat. The soup he gave me a whole bowl of. The soup I'm now sitting in.

When we moved in Logan polished an empty paint tin left over from decorating till it shone like brass and this is where our bath soaps are. It sits on the bath filled with brightly coloured bars that look fruity but just smell soapy. They don't make bubbles either. I select an apple green bar and lift it, surprised as ever by how heavy it is. I stand up to rub it on my body and turn my back on Logan so he can't see my willy.

'Turn round,' he says coaxingly, as if trying to photograph a shy girl at her birthday party. 'Ah bet yer wee brother's bigger than that awready.'

I wash my face just so I can close my eyes for a second and not see him. I feel for the bath edges and carefully lower myself to rinse my face. When I open them he's standing right over me smiling. How did he get from sitting down to standing right there without me hearing? I don't have time to work it out.

'Ye forgot to rinse yer hair,' he says, putting both hands on my head and plunging me down.

I gulp in hot soapy water and try not to swallow. I'm tall for my age but still my feet don't touch the other end of the bath. I thrash and kick but I've nothing to push against. I windmill my skinny pointless arms but they just slide down. I start to swallow when I feel myself pulled up and out into the air by my hair. I spit the water out and gasp, gulping in hot steamy air, then he pushes me under again. This time I swallow so much water I retch when he pulls me out and I think now he'll stop because he can see it's not a game any more and I really can't breathe but no . . . He pushes me down and under again and this time I stop kicking my feet and stop waving my arms. I let air and some small vital part of myself bubble out from my lips and play dead like in films. Only I can't for very long. Panic tingles in my fingers and toes which I know will betray me. If I move he'll know I'm alive and then he'll really kill me but if he thinks I am dead he might let me go and then I can come up for air and . . . He twists my hair in both hands and hauls me right up and out and drops me on the pink bathroom mat. He takes clean pressed jammies, Spider Man ones, off the towel rail and tosses them on top of me. I stay stiller than the saints in chapel. The vinyl floor is soaking and the mat squelches with sucked-up water.

'That's better,' he says, matter-of-fact as my mum finishing the dishes.

I am breathing again. Sitting on the wet mat I pull one leg into the jammies and then the other. I stand up to pull them past my bum. I put the jacket on and button it up leaving the top button undone so I can breathe. He steps forward and I flinch, closing my eyes. Tenderly he does that button up.

'Wan word,' he whispers, 'an yer wee sister's next for a bath.'

4

'Being powerful is like being a lady. If you have to tell people you are, you aren't.'

Margaret Thatcher, *The Downing Street Years*

MARY THE CANARY LIVES in a cloud of perfume and colours. She's an auxiliary nurse by day and a country and western singer by night: bed pans and power ballads. She's so glamorous she makes Mrs Hart look plain. She is the other woman and I'm being trained to hate her even though I've never met her.

My mum, my auntie Louisa and Granny Mac can't stop talking about Rosemary Murray: 'Mary the Canary'. She's been spotted coming and going from 25 Ardgour Place by Leena next door and new furniture has been delivered. She's the lipsticked cat-nailed everything my mum is not. My mum's never worn a skirt but Mary is never seen in trousers, never mind the tight snow-wash jeans my mum loves. Her feet are always crammed into what Granny Mac calls 'helter-skelters' – five-inch heels that boost her to all of five foot five. It's like her legs were made for standing on and being admired. Her ash-blonde curls, glistening with Elnett, hover a further five inches above her head. I am dying to meet this 'dolly bird', gripped by her glamour, but I can't let on.

The flat is full of bottles and nappies for Baby Billy, who is always dressed in the red, white and blue of Rangers, Logan's football team. Teenie has just started at Keir Hardie so I walk her to and from school every day holding her hand, which she hates more than me. All we talk about is our dad and how our mum still loves him even if she can't show it because of Logan. We refuse to believe she doesn't love him any more. We can't comprehend this betrayal so we smother her with reports of all the lovely things we do on custody weekends: the Strawberry Mivvis, the trips to the video shop to pick whatever we want, the going to bed without a bath. 'He'll spoil you,' she warns. But we've yet to lay eyes on Mary the Canary.

'Bottle blonde,' she huffs, furiously bleaching the inside of a teapot that we'll all taste later. 'Pound Shop Dolly Parton. Midden. Hoor's handbag,' she curses into the suds before shooshing me for asking what a 'hoor' is.

My dad has custody every second Friday from 4 p.m. and the court says he's got to return us by 4 p.m. on the Sunday. I feel like a prized library book. Friday is the only day I run home from school because I know Logan won't be there – like Jesus and God, my dad and him can't be in the same place at the same time. With every step my book-filled schoolbag bounces up and down, bruising my hip, but I don't mind because I'm going to see my dad tonight! I'm going to see my dad! I sing the words out loud, trailing Teenie behind me; I run along the road I know he'll be driving down soon and imagine him racing beside me and letting me win.

I arrive back at 1 Magdalene Drive, Carfin, panting. Teenie is right behind me. My mum thinks I'm having an asthma attack and runs for my 'puffer'. My inhaler is the very latest in weedy boy technology: it's a rigid see-through plastic bottle like the cocktail shaker in the James Bond films I watch with my dad at Christmas. Obediently I wheeze all the way out till I feel empty and dizzy then my mum makes it puff and I suck in the swimming-baths cloud, trying not to cough. I can't open my mouth or the medicine will escape like a genie so I roll my eyes up and down to show I'm OK. Sometimes I sneak a puff and pretend I'm blowing smoke rings. Still holding my breath I turn and run to my bedroom, empty my schoolbag and stuff it with pants, socks and jammies.

'It's not a holiday, Damy,' my mum shouts from the scullery.

All the kids in the flats and at school call me 'Gaymian' and 'Dame Barr' and 'Barbie'. I don't know what all the words mean but I know how they're said, know they're meant to hurt me and they do. I run and tell her and she says ignore them, they're cruel, they're stupid. She never says they're wrong. She's the only person in the world who calls me 'Damy' and I love her for that.

'Ye've still got some things at yer daddy's.'

Maybe she's left some things there too? I smile triumphantly.

Teenie is napping by the time my dad pulls up, late again, hunched over his steering wheel; this car, like all cars, too small for him. Once he drove a Mini with his head out the sun-roof. He pips the horn. My mum flicks the scullery light on and off and walks me to the front door, pulling me into my duffel coat. I wonder if they arranged these signals or if they just acted together without talking like they always did before. Teenie is limp with sleep but I'm big enough to carry her now and for once my bigness feels useful as I go carefully down the steps and over to my dad who's opened the back door for us. I can feel my mum watching us from the dark scullery window so I can't look too excited because I know this will somehow hurt her feelings. When my back is turned I crack a massive grin at my dad which he shoots right back with a 'Sssshhht' so we don't wake Teenie.

The red Ford Escort with its racy black spoiler streaks up the road to 25 Ardgour Place, Newarthill, in five minutes flat. As we slow down the familiar rhythm wakes my sister who, for once, doesn't cry. She knows my dad is there and he picks her up as easily as she would a doll if she wasn't such a tomboy. I bring the videos he's rented for us, clunking in their cases.

Using his spare hand my dad turns the back-door handle and I expect an annoyed pause as he realises it's locked and has to fumble in his pocket for the key. But no, the door opens. Strange new smells slip out.

'There's somebody I want yous to meet,' says my dad, standing my sister down.

Like Jack's magic beanstalk, Teenie tendrils herself around his leg, her head just by his knee. I'm looking around the scullery and it's cleaner than it's been since my mum left but not as clean as she likes it. There are new things on the bunker – Parmesan cheese, salad cream and coleslaw, fancy things my mum passes in the Fine Fayre. There's a big round mirror where the cork board with dentist's appointments goes. I am taking all this in when she appears.

'Ah'm Mary,' she says and it's like a film just started in my head.

Her hair is the blondest and biggest I've ever seen, bigger than Maggie's even. Teenie is still clinging to my dad's leg so I extend one hand for both of us. Her nails reach me before the rest of her fingers and I wonder how she peels tatties.

'Well, aren't we the little gent,' she says, flashing Bambi eyes at my dad. From somewhere inside her a tiny laugh escapes and it reaches me on a powerful waft of perfume I've never smelled before.

I look down at her feet bulging just slightly from bright yellow high heels pressing into the faux terracotta linoleum my mum chose so carefully. She leaves a strange but familiar footprint.

'Come on through,' she says, like we don't live there any more. And I realise we don't.

Our living room has gone. All that's left from before is Charlie sitting on the swing in his cage. I dash over to make sure it's really him, that he's not been replaced by another lesser canary, and I know it's still him because he smiles at me. We're in this together, I tell him telepathically. Teenie is now standing on my dad's foot so he swings her through on his leg. She's not said a word but doesn't need to.

A tubular chrome dining table with a smoked-glass top and six seats around it gleams where the old wooden fold-out stood. Who is going to sit here? Gone is the brown-and-orange three-piece suite and glowing anew is white leatherette with steel-inlaid arms that promise to feel cold against your arms and legs. The walls are white, white, white! The psyche-delic carpet and the orange rug the shape and colour of the sun are nowhere to be seen. We appear to be wading through a pool of blood.

'It's American Shadow,' announces Mary proudly, sweeping her hand. 'It matches ma nails. Very eighties. Yer daddy loves it, don't you, Glenn?'

I flinch, hearing my dad's name used. Mary makes us wash our hands as if our mum didn't teach us and sits us all down at the table before cramming her nails into oven gloves to rescue a bubbling dish which she plonks on a placemat, another new thing. Strings of cheese stretch from dish to plate as Mary serves my dad, then me, then Teenie. Mary shakes something that smells like feet over my plate.

'It's Parmesan,' she says in a 'take your medicine' tone. 'For your lass-agne.' 'Lass', like a girl, and 'agne', like one half of Cagney and Lacey.

After a few mouthfuls she asks if we like 'nouvelle cuisine' and we nod because it really does beat watery tatties and greasy mince – my mum loves us but she doesn't love cooking and cooking really doesn't love her. Our big colour telly, the only other survivor, stays dark.

Mary finishes her tiny portion of lasagne and gets up to put an LP on the new stereo unit. 'My coat of many colours,' she trills in time with Dolly Parton, and Charlie hops from perch to perch. When we're sure she's going to sing the whole song we all stop eating to watch and she takes to a stage only she can see. My dad can't take his eyes off her. None of us can. She finishes right along with Dolly and while the record crackles round to the next song we cannot help but clap our hands, even Teenie. Next up it's '9 to 5' and Charlie sings too and Mary grabs my dad and they're dancing. He never danced with my mum, not even when she threatened to jump on his 'two left feet', and here he is dancing with this Mary and he's rubbish and I'm mortified but I want to dance too and then Teenie gets up and we're all out of breath and our lasagne must be cold.

When the next song starts Dolly is spelling out a word letter by letter like my mum taught me on the floor of this very room with her Mills & Boons. I'm the best reader in my class and I've got my library card already. 'D-I-V-O' and my mind is racing to the end of the word Mary and Dolly are singing when my dad shouts 'MARY!' and nearly hits her as he lunges at the stereo pushing the arm off the record just as Dolly says 'R-C-E'.

Aside from the hissing speakers the room is as silent as the glass topping the table. Charlie sits more still than his wee plastic pal.

'Glenn, ye'll scratch the record,' says Mary and my dad says nothing then really cheerfully, 'Right who's for a video?' and me and Teenie cheer because somebody needs to make some noise.

I smile at Mary because nobody likes being in trouble and I don't know what she's done wrong but I don't want her to be sad. She's pretty and she's only trying to be nice. 'I like yer singing,' I whisper and she kisses me on my lips and I'm sure she's left a mark.

That night I sleep in a new bed in my old room but the house sounds different. I don't know where I expected her to sleep but Mary is in my mum's bed. I can hear her laughing her little laugh next door and my dad is low thunder through the walls. I can't get to sleep and neither can Teenie cos the door opens and light cracks in from the landing as she sneaks in my bed. Humming a tune from earlier we both fall asleep.

As usual, my dad has started his day shift long before we're up so Mary's taken the day off to look after us. Breakfast is more exotic fare: Ski Yoghurt. I snap up the Black Cherry and the Strawberry and Teenie has Vanilla. There's no sign of a teapot and I remember my mum taking it when she left.

'This is a Nescafé household now,' announces Mary. Sophistication! She unscrews the lid from the coffee jar just like the woman in the advert. It's like she stepped out the telly.

It's not even 9 a.m. and she's in full war paint, as Granny Mac would say. I make a note to report back. Mary is the enemy and I mustn't forget this. Handing me a teaspoon she invites me to pop the paper seal on the jar. It's the sound of money. Mary spoons the granules into mugs and pours boiling water over before handing us one each. I worry it might too hot for 'the wean' as she hates to be called, reminding us all she's nearly five. But Mary's not bothered so I'm not either. We sit at the brand-new breakfast bar sipping coffee and feeling grown-up. When the excitement is over we realise we're all just swinging our legs waiting for my dad to get home. Saturday suddenly seems longer than Sunday.

My mum never lets us watch videos in the daytime but Mary does. We watch *The Care Bears Movie* while Mary sits in the hall talking on the phone, which my mum never uses unless it's an absolute emergency. She's blethering away and I nip Teenie and she cries and Mary bangs the door shut. It's nearly lunchtime.

'Yees've just had yer breakfasts,' she huffs, trotting to the fridge in heels. Light from the fridge bathes her in a spotlight before she gets a can of soup down out the cupboard. 'Ah've got tae watch ma figure,' she says, patting her waist. Today she's in a floaty fuchsia skirt with a matching long-sleeved blouse and low, low neckline. 'I'll need to git yer daddy to git me wan ae they micrawaves,' she says. 'Ah've not got time for all this cooking.'

The contents of the can plop can-shaped into a pot which she plonks on to the cooker. She has to look at the front to see which ring to light. The ignition sparks and sparks before catching. After our soup we need something else to do so it's time for colouring in. Teenie scrawls and I try and fail to stay in the lines. None of my books are here so I can't read and there are no other books in the house, my mum took all her Mills & Boons. Mary is in the scullery singing away to Dolly Parton who is crying about the coat of many colours that her momma gave to her.

A head full of curlers appears around the door. 'In yees come,' she says. 'Come and see how it's done.'

I take Teenie's felt tips and put the lids on so they don't stain the new carpet and drag her into the scullery. A purple satin bag with a gold butterfly clasp spills tiny jars and bottles and brushes on to the breakfast bar. I reach out to touch what looks like a tiny light sabre and Mary smacks my hand.

'Don't touch! They're curling tongs, son.'

My cheeks burn. I'm not her son. She's not my mum. But still, she's trying and maybe I could like her then I hate myself for even having that thought.

'Shall we glam up those lovely blonde locks?' She advances towards Teenie with the tongs.

Having said nothing to Mary beyond 'please' and 'thank you' my sister now just opens her mouth and screams – screams like Mary had burnt her with the tongs. Mary jumps back and goes white under her foundation.

I just laugh. 'It's all right,' I say, addressing her adult-to-adult. 'She's funny with strangers.'

Teenie's almost white-blonde hair is always bobbed and shoved behind an ear. She's better at being a boy than me. My mum's given up buying her dresses, stopped presenting her with dollies.

'She's like that Jodie Foster,' says Mary disapprovingly. 'In *Taxi Driver*. That Robert De Niro?'

I nod and smile. Who?

Mary lifts a tickly-looking make-up brush. 'Mibbe some blusher?' Teenie shakes her head tightly. Mary looks disappointed and I feel bad for her.

'Do me,' I say, jumping up on the stool.

'Aaaaalrighty,' drawls Mary in a fake but really good fake American accent.

I sit still like one of Teenie's long-abandoned dolls and try not to flinch as she stabs a sharp black pencil at my eyes.

'They're the windaes of the soul,' says Mary. 'And windaes need dressin'.'

My eyelids are pulled towards her as she drags the mascara brush through my lashes then I make a kissing pout as she puts my lipstick on. A wrinkled nose and a sneeze as the big blusher brush dusts my face. My hair is not as naturally blond as Teenie's or as unnaturally blonde as Mary's but it's page-boy long and thick. Dry heat scorches my scalp but Mary is careful not to burn me as she works her way round my head. I cough and wheeze as she sprays what must be a whole can of Elnett and I think of Granny Mac blasting flies in her scullery.

'Done,' she says, spinning the stool round to the mirror.

I am not me. I turn my head from side to side. I look just like her. Even Teenie is a bit impressed. Maybe now my dad will want to see me more! FLASH! Mary snaps a Polaroid of her and me looking in the mirror. She shakes the picture into life and our ghost clown faces loom out. I love the attention Mary has brushed, tonged and smoothed on to me.

'Right,' she says. 'Yees better have yer bath before yer daddy gets home fae the Craig.'

I touch my face. All that work gone to waste.

Me and Teenie share a bath and it feels a shame to wash it all off. We stand on the mat – also new and also scarlet

– waiting for Mary to dry us. She handles us at arm's length like fragile, or dangerous, objects.

As she's towelling me she lets out another of her small laughs. 'Somebody takes after ees daddy,' she giggles, puffs talcum powder between my legs.

We're sat in our jammies and Mary is putting another lasagne on the table when the back door opens and cold air rushes in with my dad. We run to him and jump up and there's no mum to stop us getting dirty from his work clothes as he cuddles us both at the same time. Mary waits her turn, her face painted on.

'Honey, I'm home,' sing-songs my dad in a bad fake American accent and I notice make-up on the ends of his stubble where she kisses him.

Dad sits at the table wolfing his dinner down while Mary eats him with her eyes and I'm scared there'll be none left for us.

When he's done he drops on the puffy leather couch and it lets out a little fart. Mary clicks the telly on then kicks her helter-skelters off and curls up next to him. The skin on the soles of her feet is hard and thick and yellow. She reaches down the side of couch and fishes out something that looks like a hairbrush and hands it to my dad who starts rubbing it on her feet without taking his eyes off the telly. Each stroke shaves a small heap off. Parmesan. Me and Teenie share an armchair. My dad smiles at us as the telly warms up.

'Glenn, we'll need to get wan wae a remote control,' says Mary, fluffing herself up.

Mansions and helicopters and trilling flutes and dah-dah-dahs and men in bow ties and women dripping with diamonds and Blake and Krystle and that bitch Alexis all announce *Dynasty*.

'Dad, Dad.' I start asking the questions I always ask when he gets in from work. 'How many tons?'

And he starts giving me the answers he always gives: how much coal he fed into the furnaces and how much steel he made and I nod, seeing him riding on top of a giant JCB with a cabin big enough for him to sit up straight. He's still worried about the miners and people saying the Craig will go next and I nod along.

'Shsssht!' hisses Mary, pointing at the telly. She pushes her foot harder against the grater and the pile of shavings mounts up. '*Dynasty*!'

'So wit did yous two get up to the day, eh?' asks Dad and Mary pokes him with her painted toes.

Teenie starts telling him about colouring in and shows him a picture that he agrees looks just like him. More nodding from me.

'And wit about you eh, Professor Plum? Mair books?'

Mary moans. 'Glenn, it's *Dynasty*!' He gives her a look I don't understand and she changes her face and says, 'Oh we had a lovely time, didn't we, son?' Again with the 'son'.

I smile but need her to get her eyes off me. I head into the scullery for a glass of water I don't need. Walking past the bin I spy a packet sticking out. I pull it out and read 'Findus Lasagne'.

'It's home-cooked, not home-made,' says Mary behind me as she takes the packet out my hands and stuffs it back in the bin, deeper this time. 'Now let's make yer daddy a wee coffee and then we'll all watch *Dynasty* in peace,' she says and as she reaches up to get the jar from the cupboard her top falls open and spilling over her lacy pink bra are things my mum definitely doesn't have. Here's Dolly.

Mary catches me looking and I blush. Between the pink of her bra and the peach of her skin a small white triangle peeks out. I angle my head and move closer so I can see. She's taking an awful long time getting the jar down and as she leans forward the triangle gets bigger. It's that Polaroid. She pats it gently. I can't let my dad see it. She looks down at me. Her make-up is smiling.

That night I'm woken up by banging. I don't have to strain to hear Mary's chorus through the wall: 'Oh Glenn! Oh Glenn!'

I cry bitter, jealous tears into my pillow.

5

'I cannot offer you an easy road; you would not expect
that of me.'

Margaret Thatcher, first Speech to Conservative
Central Council, 15 March 1975

T HE SIPPY IS A powdery patch of the moon down here
on earth. The old cement works is the short cut from
Carfin to Newarthill and because I never, ever want to go
back to that flat I never, ever take it. Instead I walk back from
Keir Hardie Memorial Primary School in baby-steps heel-
to-toe and for every three forward I take one back. This way
I'm always the last one left on the road. I feel the looks from
passing cars. Don't you have a home to go to?

The Sippy made the giant hour-glass cooling towers for
the Craig, where my dad says clouds are made. Like the Bing
and the Craig, the Sippy is totally man-made but where the
Bing is sparkling black mountains the Sippy is a chalky tundra
the size of however many football pitches. All that remains is
the sign saying *SIPAREX CEMENT WORKS*, the chain-
link fence round the site that lets you see in and the rust-sealed
padlock on the spiky front gates. There's nothing else. It's as
if the workers took their factory away brick by brick at the
end of their last shift.

All the action here is underground.

Take the deepest breath you can and pinch your nose hard so you don't smell the pish when you run down the deep, dark stairs with the slippery chalky walls that leave the tips of your fingers damp white. Keep your eyes closed if you want because you won't see a thing unless you're starting a fire or somebody stole a torch. Blink as fast as you can, your eyes won't suck in more light. You're inside the world now and all you can smell is broken rocks and something else, something musty and exciting. These forgotten cellars are perfect for doing the things you don't want to get caught doing. This is where girls come to get poked off and watch boys smoke. It's not for good boys like me, boys with a geeky galaxy of gold stars.

It's about a mile from Flat 1, 1 Magdalene Drive, Carfin, to the gates of Keir Hardie Memorial Primary School, Newarthill. The two villages are linked by a long road that goes on down the brae to the Craig and then to Motherwell town centre. This is my dad's road to work and I imagine his car hitting me and me bouncing over the bonnet and tears trickling down his nose on to my face keeping me alive like a fairy-tale princess till the ambulance comes.

My mum worries about me and Teenie getting run over on the dark mornings – she says Maggie's trying to put the clocks backwards or forwards or something so the English can all have a lie-in and all the mums are raging because it means we're all going to get splatted walking to school. To stop this happening we must all learn the Green Cross Code. We file on to the school stage which doubles as the television room and the curtains are pulled and the hinged doors of the TV cabinet fold back. We sit cross-legged in rows, shortest at the front and tallest, me, at the back. The telly is gigantic and it takes a minute to warm up while Miss Wills rewinds the video. When the Green Giant comes on I imagine sleeping on his big broad chest in the tight white vest with the big green cross on, rising and falling as he breathes in and out. That afternoon a policeman comes to class and we all consider our crimes quietly. Officer Leighton – my middle name, maybe we're related – is wearing a short-sleeved shirt, the hairs on his arms are like Weetabix covered in golden syrup. When he smashes one fist into the other to demonstrate the impact of a car on a child the muscles and tendons flex and dance and the hairs sparkle in the sun.

We're each allocated an older boy or girl to walk with us and keep us off the roads. Teenie gets one of the six more or less identical Cullen sisters, all with the long black hair that their mum, the Bonny Tress, spends all Sunday after chapel washing and brushing till it shines. I get dumped on Kevin McAdam two years above me. His hair is the colour of hay in a Ladybird book about farms. Kev probably didn't read that book or any book. He sits like lead at the bottom of his class. He does boxing and judo because he's too big to be a karate kid. I hate fighting, can't fight, but I can nearly do the standing-crane thing, arms outstretched, if I don't look down. I dream of taking off. I've got the right build for karate but the wrong lungs. Because judo is really just throwing your weight it's perfect for Kev. I stick to reading whatever I can find and wheezing and taking the Brer Rabbit route out of trouble. Kev is always surrounded by boys and I'm always running away from them. When the big yellow Library Bus comes round once a fortnight I sit on the corrugated-rubber floor reading until it's time for it to go somewhere else and when it rolls off Kev and his pals egg it.

I'm scared it won't come back but it does. I think about hiding on it and running away.

The McAdams stay on the second floor in the block of flats opposite. Me and my mum and Teenie and Baby Billy and Logan stay at Flat 1, 1 Magdalene Drive, which makes us number one in all the flats. Baby Billy has blond hair and blue eyes and smiles for everybody. He has a sterling silver teething ring and everybody who visits brings him christening money. Me and Teenie aren't really sure what to do with him. Logan likes to remind us he's only our half-brother. We're never allowed to pick him up and Logan keeps him near. Billy gets disposable nappies – no danger of a pinprick for him, less work for my mum. Billy is a quiet baby, 'Quieter than both of yours,' we're reminded. Sometimes I read him stories. I try to see my face in his.

Because we're on the ground floor I really do look up to Kev and wish his bedroom was at the front so I could watch him do his judo practice. He harrumphs across the road and sulks at the bottom of our front steps.

My mum's reading the *Daily Record*.

'Och, wit a waste of a man,' she wails. She breathes in a confidential way. 'Me and yer daddy went tae see him at the pictures when we were courtin'. You'd never have guessed.'

Guessed what? The offending paper is binned as if contagious. I snatch it out the bin when she's busy with the toast. Rock Hudson is dead. I've learnt to decode the signals in the papers: 'flamboyant', 'confirmed bachelor', 'troubled'. They all mean one thing.

When it's time to leave my mum's fussing over me like it's my first day again, spitting on her hand and rubbing it over my cow's lick, trying to make my hair stay down. I shake her off but Kev's already seen. I'm nine and nearly as tall as her. Kev's face says he's not thrilled about being stuck with me but our mums are best pals so he'll have to do as he's told.

'Taken a beamer, Barr.' He laughs at my blushes as my mum kisses me at the front door.

'Yous two are not too old to hold hands,' she shouts from the top step.

Now Kev turns red. He crushes my hand into his, throwing it down as soon as we're round the corner. My hand tingles as blood flows back into my fingers as he storms ahead and I delight in the trouble he'll be in if I do get run over. After ten minutes he stops at the Sippy gates and folds his arms waiting for me to catch up.

Just as I reach him he disappears behind a tree whose fuzzy grey buds are breaking into dangling yellow catkins. They sway like Mary's earrings. I stare at the branchy place where Kev was and his head reappears.

'Pish!' he says, rubbing his crotch. 'Move!'

I carefully push the branches out of my face, wary of twangings back and scratchings. I'm so busy trying to escape the tree I nearly walk straight into Kevin's hot, steaming jet. He laughs then focuses on arcing through the fence mixing with the grey powdery cement dust that covers the whole Sippy to make a minging yellow paste. He aims like a soldier and I wonder what enemy he sees. I try not to look or look like I'm not looking. Effortlessly, he chucks his bag over the fence past his pish. I worry about his books before clicking that he's not got any. Now no one can see us from the road. I panic. Kev isn't rushing to school, he's just trying to fit in fun on the way. He doesn't care that we'll get in trouble if we're caught. I've never dogged school or smoked a fag. I've never even been late. 'He's for the uni,' my mum tells women up the high street. 'He'll be Dr Barr one day, you wait and see.' Every certificate of excellence or – gasp, mere merit – is framed. Every report card is read aloud to any neighbour with five minutes to spare or not. This year it said, 'Damian tends towards the talkative.' I've started talking back, not a lot but a bit – I'm bored, there's never enough to read and if I make everybody laugh then I'm not Gaymian for that minute. Now I'm in the Sippy with a judo black belt two years above me. I can't talk my way out of whatever we're up to and for the first time I'm not sure I want to.

With two hands Kev pulls up the bottom of the chain-link fence and it folds in a familiar way. 'Through!'

I drop down and wriggle under commando-style, not thinking about the stains on my uniform – the charcoal-grey trousers, white shirt and burgundy blazer with burgundy and sky-blue diagonally striped tie. He boots my bum as I make it through but not hard.

Grey world, grey half-light of a see-your-breath morning in early March. The Council daffodils are still sleeping in their buds. It's half past eight and orange streetlights burn filthily on the road we just left. The Sippy has not one light, not one in the whole place. Somehow Kev knows where he's going and I blindly follow, fitting my feet into the prints he leaves in the grey dust. One small step.

'Watch it!' He swerve-jumps left and I only just follow and we both miss a hole that goes down how far nobody knows. A hole made for falling into.

Dust swirls the surface of the Sippy, camouflaging these staircases with no stairs and these shafts that have lost their lifts. Luke falls into the ice cave in *The Empire Strikes Back* and defeats the razor-clawed Hoth Wampa. I'd probably find a pissy tramp, if I was lucky.

Just because he can, Kev sprints ahead and I follow him as fast as I can, diving under the fence at the other side and dusting myself down as I run huffing and puffing through the school gates shouting 'Thanks' but I'm not sure what for. Kev doesn't look back. He ignores me at playtime and he ignores me at dinnertime and only when everybody else has been picked up after the last bell does he come and get me for our walk home through the Sippy.

My mum's delighted I've not been run over so from now on Kev has to walk me to and from school. Suits me. Nobody slags me off with Kev there because if I go home crying or bleeding he'll get in trouble. Teenie's stuck with one of the Cullen girls who's learned the hard way she's not interested in having her hair plaited.

Every day before and after school, when Logan's out in his British Gas van, I beg my mum to get back with my dad. I start politely but it always ends with tears and why, why, why.

She turns away. 'Yer daddy's got Mary the Canary now anyway.'

On custody weekends I beg my dad when Mary's in the bath but he warns off the waterworks: 'She's made her bed and she can lie in it and that's that.' He turns the telly up.

Whenever our dad is late or doesn't show up for custody Teenie has an excuse: an extra shift, a car problem, some-thing, anything. I let her believe them. I play with the girls and she plays with the boys but I'm still her big brother. When boys knock the door it's her they want on their team for football or whatever but it's my bed she crawls in when she wakes up from the nightmares she has now. She never cries during the day. I do. I cry all the time. 'She's mair man than you,' Logan likes to say. He only hits Teenie once, a big juicy slap round her face – his hand nearly bigger than her head. I don't know why, I never know why, but she hits him straight back, a kick in the shins, and he laughs and that's that.

For all of Primary Five me and Kev cut through the Sippy. One day, when the tree by the gate is green with leaves, I get back and my auntie Louisa is standing in the scullery where my mum should be. I taste the air for Logan. He's not here.

'It's just me,' she says, too cheerful, and I breathe out but not all the way.

She's banging doors looking for things in unfamiliar cupboards. I try helping but she shooshes me out the way. Teenie is outside playing football, I can hear her out the scullery window.

'Where's Mum?' I ask, trying to sound like I don't think there's anything wrong. Auntie Louisa stops fussing with pots but keeps her back to me. Louder: 'Where's my mum?' She doesn't turn or speak. 'Auntie Louisa. Where's. My. Mum?' I sound each word the way adults do when they really need you to answer.

She turns round and she's crying and I'm shocked she's been crying without any noise.

'She's away, son.'

'Away? Away where?'

'Glasgow.'

I stare at her. Glasgow is a million miles away. How did she get there? Why is she not here? What's in Glasgow?

'She's at the hospital.'

Hospital. I relax. There must be another baby, a brother or a sister, but she didn't look fat this time and where is Baby Billy anyway? I can't hear him in the flat.

'She's at the hospital in Glasgow, Damian, son. She's not well. She's had a . . .'

I start crying and don't bother to be quiet about it.

'Now don't cry, son, she'll be all right. C'mon, no greetin'. She went in a helicopter. A helicopter, Damy!'

She called me 'Damy'. Only my mum calls me that. What if she never gets to call me 'Damy' again? All I can think is how my mum hates planes and how when she went to Kitty Smith's wedding in Belgium she went all the way there and back on a train and a boat.

'C'mon, be brave for yer auntie, that's it, c'mon, son.' She cuddles me and I'm crying but I'm not crying for my mum, well not just for her. I'm crying for me and Teenie left here with him but maybe . . .

'So do we go back to my dad's now?' I ask, jagging, stuttering over the words but already hopeful.

'No, son . . . yer daddy's busy with work. He's not got room for yous.'

'He has so.'

I know he's got room – there's one spare room in 25 Ardgour Place, two if you count the one Mary the Canary turned into a dressing room for all her rhinestones. She's doing well with her singing, doing more gigs in clubs than shifts at the hospital. My dad doesn't like her staying out late, doesn't like that she sometimes comes home with flowers, doesn't like that she likes Lambrusco.

'Yer daddy's not got room so I'm goin' tae come in and see yous both and Big Brenda over the road's going tae watch yous and Billy's goin' tae his granny's. Yer mammy'll be fine, son. She will. She's a tough wee bird. She's got the Lord. She's not gonnae die.'

Die? DIE?! Nobody mentioned dying. Dying. Until now I never thought my mum would ever die and she sees this in my face and turns to the sink.

'These tatties'll not peel themselves, go and play wi yer wee sister and don't upset her.'

Next morning and every morning Kev's mum, Big Brenda, gets me and Teenie ready for school. She's Irish and she always smells of stewed tea and she prays under her breath and tells us to make our mammy proud at school. I ask what's wrong with my mum and she says something about a 'hem-reej' and I ask her to spell it so I can look it up in the class dictionary but she can't. It's to do with her brain and we're all to pray for her. Logan is never in when Auntie Louisa or Big Brenda is. When he gets home from work I run out to play as far away as I can – I hide on the Library Bus, I sit on the swings at the swing-park reading, maybe join in a game of tig with the Cullen girls, if they'll let me play. I draw the line at letting them do my hair in their Sindy salon but only cos they'll tell everybody I let them put curlers in. When Logan shouts us in for the night I sneak in the front door then stay in my room with the door shut, pretending to sleep.

Everybody is nicer to me and Teenie now our mum's in the hospital. The pitying looks we get are better than dirty divorce looks. Only Kev treats me just the same.

Every day he pishes in his favourite place. I'm always careful to go before but this one time I'm bursting so I stand next to Kev and close my eyes and finally it flows. I open my eyes again and try not to look at him or look like I'm not looking. He's aiming his piss at some invisible enemy, I can tell. His cock is more grown-up than his Teenage Mutant Ninja Turtle pants and he shakes it and I shake my smaller, balder effort and we adjust our flannels. I pick my bag up and am nearly at the fence when I miss Kev. He's disappeared. I look around and then from under the ground: 'C'mon, Barr! Come on down!'

What is this? *The Price Is Right?* My dad loves that programme, loves a gamble. Kev's voice echoes below. I know all the hidey-holes down here now or thought I did when his hand waves from a hatch about five feet away. How did I miss that? I sit on the edge and I'm bracing myself to drop into the darkness when Kev grabs my legs and pulls me down. It's a uniform-ruining slide down into chalky-glowing blackness.

'Kevin?' A seashell silence. 'Kev?' I echo.

'Over here, Barr.'

I move towards his voice with hands stretched in front like a zombie.

My fingers find him first and wordlessly he slides them down the front of his shirt to his snake belt which is jingling undone. His breath ruffles my hair. He pushes my hands past his waistband and I feel hair – hair down there. Breathing deeply he wraps my hand around his cock still wet with piss and hard, so hard.

'Pull!' So I pull it like a Christmas cracker. He smacks my head. 'You tool. Like this,' and he takes my hand in his like we're walking to school and shows me what he wants.

The faster I go the faster he breathes and after a minute he kind of gasps then straight away pulls my hand out his pants and shakes me off and I don't know what I've done wrong.

'Right,' he says, clicking his belt closed. He ghosts past in the dark then takes a run and clambers up and I know he's going to leave me here. He reaches down. 'C'mon, hame time!'

I grab my schoolbag and take his hand and scrabble up blinking into the world. I'm half in, half out when Kev says what he'll do to me if I tell, which bones he'll break, and I'm surprised how much biology he knows. I promise I won't tell, even in my prayers, especially not in my prayers. It's not even four o'clock. We'll be home in time for *He-Man and the Masters of the Universe*. I look down at my trousers and there's something like egg white on the legs and it must be chalk off the walls so I brush it but it smears so I just leave it.

Kev walks ahead as usual but maybe not quite so far and I see Teenie skipping ropes with her pals and I'm in the front door of the flat earlyish for a change and there's Logan. No Auntie Louisa, no Big Brenda and still no Mum. I feel my face fall but try to stop it because it's worse if I look scared.

'Here,' he says matter-of-factly, pointing to an invisible spot right in front of him.

I drop my bag by the door and walk over, eyes down. He gets down in front of me and I can see the top of his head, his scalp raw under his curly coppery hair. He's sniffing at my trousers, loud so I know he's sniffing like the Child Catcher in *Chitty Chitty Bang Bang*.

He stands up and without a word grabs me by my school tie and I'm dangling in the air kicking my legs and choking not screaming and he boots opens my bedroom door and throws me in. My palms burn as I skid on the brown-cord carpet. I start crawling away but he plucks me up by my ears and flings me on to my bed.

'Fuckin' jessy!' He spits at me but hits the bed. 'Dirty fuckin' fairy. I'll fuckin' show yae! Wait till yer daddy hears about you! Poofter!'

He stops shouting. Now he's muttering and looking round and round but I don't know what for and I don't think he knows and I'm saying, 'I'm sorry, I'm sorry,' but I don't know what for and he says, 'You will be.'

He stops and stares at my rocking horse, the one my dad bought me when he won on the Grand National that you're not to rock too fast on because you'll go over the front. It's creamy white with dappled brown spots and a long chestnut mane that Teenie likes to brush. She won't brush her own hair or her dollies' but she loves this horse, loves all horses.

I sit up on my bed and pull my knees up to my face and look at Logan. I know it's better to say nothing now because whatever I've done already is bad enough. He walks over to the horse gently like it might trot away and takes the brown leather reins in his hand wrapping them round and round his fist. With one hand he lifts the horse up off the floor and slowly he starts to spin round and round and I think he's going to smash it off the wall and break its beautiful legs and faster and faster and round and round and, 'They're off!' he shouts, letting go of the reins and that's the last of my baby teeth.

Kev says nothing about my gappy smile, none of the teachers ask anything. My adult teeth come in squinty and big and I start putting my hand over my mouth when I talk. We spend longer and longer at the Sippy after school and I'm careful not to get anything on my trousers again. One time Kev stole a torch off his mum and we looked in dark wet corners and found an old *Razzle* mag all crumpled and ripped and stained. We were obviously not the first to find this treasure. Who dared lift it from the top shelf at the Paki's? Kev pulls himself looking at the 'big busty blondes' that remind me of Mary the Canary and I pull myself watching him, copying him exactly, and forget all about having to go back to that flat.

Sometimes Kev crushes me in a judo hold but never that hard and only because he thinks he should really. He reminds me what he'll do if I tell. This isn't my worst secret and I don't want him to stop, any more than he wants to get caught. I keep quiet. Kev sees my bruises and is quite impressed by one or two of them. He knows I don't do judo but he doesn't say anything. I pray for my mum to come home every night but every day I wake up and she's still not there. Even if she was I wouldn't tell her because I don't want to upset her, especially now she's not well. My dad thinks boys should have bruises. Logan says nobody will believe me anyway and Teenie will get it if I tell. Sometimes at school I put my hand up and open my mouth to tell the teacher everything but all that comes out is answers. Nobody asks the right questions. Nobody wants to know.

6

'. . . I place a profound belief – indeed a fervent faith – in the virtues of self-reliance and personal independence.'

> Margaret Thatcher, first Speech to Conservative
> Central Council, 15 March 1975

THE SUMMER HOLIDAYS ARE still a few weeks away but I'm already dreading them as much as the rest of Primary Five is looking forward to them. After the holidays Kev starts at Brannock High School, which they've not long finished building across the road from Keir Hardie. It's five floors high – the biggest thing around, except for the Craig. High school pupils use pens instead of pencils and walk between specialised classrooms carrying different-coloured folders for each subject. They sit exams instead of tests. Their bell rings at 3.30 p.m. – a whole extra half-hour of learning, of not being at home. So, on the dark mornings I'll be walking to and from Keir Hardie on my own. Without Kev the Sippy will be off-limits.

With her eyes raised to heaven Auntie Louisa announces that my mum is finally out of the Glasgow Southern General Hospital where she's been for the past six months. Hallelujah! But she's got to go and stay with Granny Mac till she's well enough to come home. We're still not allowed to go and see her. She needs her rest, we're told. Me and Teenie beg and plead but have to settle for making yet another *GET WELL* card, careful to make it very clear that *WE'RE OK!* I get Auntie Louisa on her own and say maybe I could visit myself if Teenie is too young and she looks like she's thinking about it but then shakes her head. Logan gets to go and see her but he doesn't take our card.

Logan has very strict rules about everything but only he knows them and they change all the time. Just when I think I've mastered eating – no clanking cutlery, no seconds, no complaining of feeling hungry – I'll chew the wrong way and . . .

Since my mum went into hospital I've been doing all her chores. Logan likes things done a certain way. He calls me 'Cinders'. Every morning before school I brush the ashes from the fireplace in the living room – we've not had fires in our bedrooms since my mum took ill. Although Logan works for the gas man we've no central heating, none of the flats have. At night in bed your breath clouds above you like dreams. Sometimes I sleep with my school uniform on and try not to move so I don't get it creased. In the morning Jack Frost's long thin fingers have scratched inside the windows.

The first morning Logan tells me to clean out the fire I put the ashes in a plastic bucket I find under the scullery sink. Some hot bits melt the plastic and I trail grey ash behind me all through the flat and out through the close to the big ash bin out the back. I Hansel-and-Gretel my way back, bracing myself, but Logan just hands me a brush and I sweep it up and that's that.

Next morning the wee brass stand that holds the brush and shovel is empty.

'Use yer hands,' says Logan, standing over me.

I start scooping the silky warm ashes up into the metal bucket he's provided and at first they feel nice like the sand on the beach at Portobello where my dad took us one weekend. But then they get hotter and soon tiny red jewels like the ends of cigarettes are stuck all over my hands and I try shaking them off but they're burnt on. If I singe the carpet I'll be in trouble. Breathing deeply through my nose without turning round or making a noise, I lift out all the ashes and fill the metal bucket. Then, careful not to rush, I twist yesterday's *Daily Record* into kindling, reading the headlines as I go. Maggie beat the miners, they say. Only when I'm outside emptying the bucket into the ash bin do I pick the now-black embers from my hands. I cry quietly because crying can turn a beating into a rattling. So you don't cry. Teenie doesn't cry much but I make sure I take any blame for her.

One Saturday morning, tired of being teased, I decide to try football again. I get the ball straight away and Teenie is staring wide-eyed and I'm thinking, 'This is easy' as I nip past Kev and the other boys and boot it straight through the two jumpers that make the goals and BOOM!

'OG!' shouts Teenie, 'own goal', and my team run at me and Teenie boots the ball away to distract them and it sails past the goal and straight through our living-room window. Before the glass finishes smashing Logan's blazing face appears. To stop Teenie running forward – the only person she can lie to is herself – I put my hand up like I'm in class and say 'My fault' and start walking to the door I know he'll be waiting behind. She's my little sister. I'm the man of the house now.

So I'm dreading days without school. I don't think Logan is looking forward to them either. One of the highlights of my week is *Dynasty*. Me and Teenie watch it every other Friday night at my dad's with him and Mary the Canary. We all hate Alexis Colby but we're quiet when she's on with her big black hair and her shoulder pads and her posh bitchy voice. We love it when she slaps dumb blonde Krystle Carrington and they throw sequins at each other before rolling into a handy mud pit.

Even my dad laughs. 'It's that far-fetched,' he says. 'But I do like the dolly birds,' and nudges me, winking at the telly. He nudges me again.

'I like her hair,' I say, pointing at Alexis. Really I only have eyes for Steven Carrington, the troubled blond with the big blue eyes.

Mary gets up to go and redo her lipstick and as she goes I notice Charlie's cage is empty. Before I can ask where he is my dad says, 'Sorry, son,' and I burst into tears. 'He flew away.' Mary doesn't look bothered, in fact she looks like Alexis Colby.

My other pleasure is *Story Teller* – the fortnightly magazine from Marshall Cavendish which comes with a cassette on the front so you can play the stories out loud and read them at the same time. I'm getting too old for it I know but I listen over and over to 'Gobbolino the Witch's Cat', 'Ford and the Cars' and 'The Wizard of Oz'. I don't use headphones so I can hear Logan if he creeps up behind me. He does that. It costs £1.95 and my dad brings me a new issue every time he picks us up.

My secret pleasure is the Majorettes: a rhinestone relic from when we had coal pits. All the pretty girls aged four to twelve, and a few fat ones, wear pink tutus and tights and little white bolero jackets and feathers on their heads and march to music twirling batons and throwing them up high. The coal's gone but the music plays on – Carfin Community Centre hasn't got a band any more so they use a ghetto blaster which goes ahead on a wheelbarrow for parades. They practise all winter and dance all summer and everybody turns out to watch like it's the Orange Walk only this doesn't end with Catholics and Protestants fighting. Anyone can be a Majorette. So long as you're a girl.

I turn up at a rehearsal. The teacher, a woman called Elaine who everybody says is a Gypsy, eyes me through her mascara. She's not unkind but explains it's not for me. I insist it is. She hands me a baton and the girls stop to stare but she orders them to carry on twirling. The baton is shiny steel, maybe from the Craig, and each end has a white rubber stopper so the baton bounces if it falls. I catch the beat, extend my hand and twirl. Once, twice, three times it goes round and as Elaine smiles I lose focus and bounce, bounce, bounce, my pride falls to the floor with the baton. A chorus of giggles. Elaine says I can watch them practise but it feels like punishment so I run away.

The last term of Primary Five is nearly over when a new teacher joins Keir Hardie. We're all appalled. We thought teachers were for ever. You start off with kind, moon-faced Miss Traynor in Primary One and work your way through to scary hairy-nostrils Mr Baker in Primary Seven before going off to Brannock High School (I got Mr Baker in Primary Four as well for some reason). But oh no. Our Miss Wills, who always let us do our work outside on sunny days, has suddenly retired and we've got this new teacher: Mrs Rayson. We decide to call her 'Rayson the Basin' because her hairdresser obviously uses a bowl to do her bob.

Every class has to say the Lord's Prayer at the start of every day but Mrs Rayson says it like she means it. Instead of reading the new Roald Dahl she opens the brown-leather *Good News Bible* with the gold cross on the front and pauses to make sure we're listening. It's not like when we walk in pairs to church at Easter and sit on a cold wooden pew listening to Mr Knowles go on and on about how we need to work hard in this life for the hereafter is not certain for sinners like us. And it's not like the 'thees' and 'thous' and bells and smells and endless standing up and kneeling down of the chapel that I used to sneak in with my mum who's barred because she's divorced. 'Jesus disnae care about a daft bit of paper,' she'd say, bowing her head to cross herself before kneeling at the back. They've all been praying for her to get better at the chapel.

Mrs Rayson's Bible is full of stories and I love them. I never want the bell to go at 3 p.m. but the clanging seems especially cruel when Daniel is in the lion's den. I need to know where Samson's Hulk strength really comes from. When she reveals that Mary Magdalene was a prostitute Amanda Ferguson shouts 'Hoor' and everybody hoots and instead of shouting Mrs Rayson gently shooshes us. She doesn't treat us like we're stupid just because we don't know something.

At the first assembly she takes, Mrs Rayson announces she'll be holding a meeting in the gym every Wednesday after school for pupils who want to find out more about Jesus. I need more stories and I'm desperate to go anywhere but home so I head along. In the farthest corner Mrs Rayson sits on a stool with the piano panting to be played behind her. Cross-legged on the floor in a circle around her are about a dozen pupils, one older than me and the rest younger. Most have specs and few have pals.

'Sit down,' says Mrs Rayson graciously.

I join the others on the gym floor tattooed with interlocking lines and circles, different colours for different games and all a mystery to me.

'Welcome to Scripture Union,' says Mrs Rayson, smiling. 'Jesus said to St Mark: I am the way, and the truth, and the life; no one comes to the Father but through Me. Through Scripture Union you will understand the word of the Lord and come to know Him and love Him just as He loves all of you.'

A huge fart vibrates through the floor before reeking through the air and the perpetrator takes a beamer. 'Even you, David Dawson,' says Mrs Rayson, her kindness stretched but not snapped.

We start off singing 'The ink is black, the page is white; together we learn to read and write,' which has a ploddingly pleasing 'da dum dum dum'. It's about how we're all the same inside. I think I'm different inside. This doesn't have much to do with Jesus and neither does the one about hammering in the morning and the evening.

Between songs Mrs Rayson reads us Bible stories which she calls lessons but they don't feel like work. She quizzes us after each one and every time my hand shoots up she looks slightly pitiful before smiling. The right answer produces a Black Jack from her miraculously bottomless handbag. Loaves and fishes. Soon my tongue is swot-black.

We learn that how we act in this life decides where we go next. Up or down. We must always speak the truth. If we're good we'll go up to heaven and if we're bad we'll go down to hell. There's no confession, no forgiveness. You can't just say you're sorry. Even if you're only two minutes late for Scripture Union Mrs Rayson makes you sit outside the circle where you can hear the stories but not feel them. We must work hard at being good, she says. That's what Maggie's always saying on the News: work harder, do more, get more.

Logan doesn't want me in the flat any more than I want to be there so he's happy for me to go to Scripture Union. 'It's not Catholic, is it?' he demands, so I get him a letter from Mrs Rayson on Scripture Union notepaper with their symbol, an Aladdin's lamp, assuring him the Pope has nothing to do with it.

Along with the rest of the world, Mrs Rayson knows about our 'broken home' and my mum being in the hospital with her haemorrhage (which I looked up in the school *Encyclopaedia Britannica*). When we all sit in a circle holding hands, praying with our eyes closed, Mrs Rayson puts in a mention for my mum and I feel a charge of sympathy in my fingers.

I love 'the word'. As for 'the truth' . . . I am desperate to tell Mrs Rayson what's happening at 1 Magdalene Drive but I'm scared no one will believe me and they'll tell Logan what I've told them and he'll smile like he does when other adults are about and ruffle my hair and wait till they've gone then kill me. I don't want Mrs Rayson to think I don't really enjoy Scripture Union because I do. I started coming as an excuse to avoid home but I really do love it now: none of the boys or girls who call me names come here, you don't have to run or catch a ball and the stories are great – we've even been awarded Gospels printed on see-through paper in tiny letters. Inside each one has our name typed neatly on a label that says

Ex Libris. But they're not library books, we don't have to give them back. And if I tell them about Logan, what about my other secrets? Do I have to tell them too? Then I'll surely go to hell. At the end of the Lord's Prayer I say a quick one in my head asking God to kill Logan and make me like girls so I won't burn in hell, Amen.

To make up for all my lies I decide to tell Mrs Rayson a truth. I hang back and when everybody else is gone I tell her that everybody calls her 'Rayson the Basin'.

'What?'

'Because of your bowl cut, miss,' I explain, drawing a circle in the air around my head.

The light goes out of her face. She stacks the song books.

'Thank you, Damian,' she says, sounding tired.

I thought she'd be pleased with the truth. Now I feel bad. 'Miss, I . . .'

'Thank you, Damian. That is all. Now, let us pray.' And we kneel down praying together, just the two of us, but I'm not sure what for.

Now it's nearly summer there's no danger of anybody getting run over. The mornings are light and even the night shines through my horrible porridge-coloured curtains well after bedtime. Not long after the sun goes down we get a second sunset here. It starts with a dull big deep boom you feel in your chest and then there's a massive clanking like God's dropped his cutlery drawer on the scullery floor and then silence as the sky glows pink then orange then red before fading back. People stand on their front steps and watch it before going back in to the telly. This show only lasts until they finish emptying the furnaces at the Craig but it's long enough to snatch a couple of sentences so I keep a Gospel under my pillow. Every night I think of my dad sitting in the cabin of the giant eight-wheeled Kress-carrier laden with buckets of white-hot steel. My dad makes the sun set twice every night and he does it just for me.

So now it's light there's no need for Kev to hold my hand. Without him I won't brave the Sippy in case there are other boys and I'm in no hurry to get back so I walk the longer way but despite baby-steps I always end up back at 1 Magdalene Drive.

Then I go to the Grotto.

Carfin Grotto is a replica of Lourdes halfway down the road between Newarthill and Carfin, just past the garage where my Dad had a stand-up argument with the man about the price of petrol. The Grotto is a massive outdoor chapel bigger than Brannock, the Fine Fayre and the Coop put together. It's all ancient like something from the Bible even though the sign says it was only built after the First World War. Nothing here is Council rough-cast, it's all stone, and all the lamps are delicate glass bowls on fancy wrought-iron stands. There's no gate, you can come or go at any time (but watch out for the beaky Canon if you're not accompanied by an adult!). Enter between two big mushroom-shaped stone turrets, leaving the tarmacked secular world behind, crunching on spiritual gravel. An outdoor altar dominates the main arena. It's like the stone table from Narnia and it would be a sin to lie on it and feel the coolness against my face but I want to. Radiating out from this are rows and rows of hundreds of white plastic chairs tipped forward so the never-ending rain runs off. Nobody wants to sit through Mass with a wet arse. Microphones and speakers are brought out for the Sunday services and you can hear the chanting for miles. Logan runs about the flat closing the windows to keep the Pope out. He turns the football up on the telly and cheers extra loud every time Rangers score – if they're winning he's happy and in these moments I feel safe. The only thing he hates more than me is Catholics. Despite her red hair and freckles and gold crucifix on a chain my mum is let off because she doesn't support Celtic or any other football team. (He doesn't know she still sneaks off to the Grotto sometimes.)

The rest of the Grotto is a series of shrines linked by carefully kept rose gardens. Each tells a Bible story. It's heaven to sit quietly at the feet of the Virgin Mary in her bright blue tea-towel robe. Pink plaster flakes from her face and surely her halo needs a touch-up from Mary the Canary with her waxy-smelling make-up bag of tricks. The Blessed Virgin stands even taller than my dad in a dazzling white alcove surrounded by yew bushes dotted with red berries. She's the star of the Grotto. This is her sanctuary.

'She turned up in a vision tae a wee Polish lassie,' whispers Granny Mac as if the Mother of Christ might be easily spooked. Striking miners built the Grotto in 1922 to immortalise this vision and every Sunday coachloads of pilgrims pile out from all over the world hoping to glimpse her. I get to see her every day. I put my schoolbag down on the gravel so the stones don't stick in my knees and pray for my mum to get better, for Mary the Canary to fly away and Logan to go to hell so my mum and dad can get back together. I peek through one eye hoping she'll creak into life like a statue from *Clash of the Titans* but she shows no sign. Not today.

In an artificial cave dripping with ivy there's a life-sized Joseph carpentering, his chisel raised in one hand for ever. It's damp in here and black mould blots his cheeks but I don't let him know I've noticed. You can see where Jesus gets his looks. Next door St John the Baptist is raising both hands to heaven, head still on. I always pick a daisy and leave it for St Theresa, who looks so depressed in that jobby-brown habit. I love all the shrines but my favourite bit of the Grotto is the gift shop.

Located by the entrance in a tiny octagonal building with a peeling, bottle-green door, the gift shop is where the pilgrims snap up souvenirs. It's open every day from 8.30 a.m. till 5.30 p.m. I am there daily from just after 3 p.m. until Jane turns the key. Jane runs the gift shop. She's older than Granny Mac, more ancient than Methuselah and her face is wrinkly like a ball-bag. But she's not witchy or scary. She's Irish like Big Brenda and laughs easily with the pilgrims who never leave without buying something. I don't talk to her the first few times in case I'm not supposed to be there. I don't even put my schoolbag down. I just stare at the holy medals, the colourful prayer cards with specific powers and the ornaments of all the saints and disciples. I love the Jesus with a light-up bleeding red heart.

One day there's no one else in the shop and Jane, laughing, asks me, 'Have you not got a home to go to?'

Staring at a long sheet of paper filled with a mess of '1's and '0's hanging on the wall behind her, I say, 'No,' then force a laugh in case she believes me and calls social services. Her wrinkles team up into a smile and she opens a drawer by the till and gets out a bag of marshmallows.

'What's your name, son?'

'Damian Leighton Barr.'

'That's a lovely name, Damian, and do you know about Father Damian who went to live among the lepers and . . .'

Every day Jane feeds me sweets and stories. Glinting under the glass-topped counters she's forever dusting are all the saints' medals. Carefully she untucks them from their velvet beds: St Jude, the patron saint of lost causes, is my favourite. Sometimes Jane is reading the *Daily Record* when I go in and we talk about how they're striking at the Craig and I tell her my dad works there and she says she'll pray for him. I'd like her to pray for me. I want to tell Jane everything, to confess.

Instead I ask her about the weird bit of paper with all the numbers on it and she giggles.

'Have you not got a computer at that Protestant school of yours?'

'Yes,' I say. She knows fine well Keir Hardie is officially non-denominational. 'We've got a computer each.' Another lie, another baby-step to hell, God forgive me.

'Squint at it,' says Jane, and I close my eyes and the mess of numbers blurs and swims and suddenly Jesus Christ is smiling out at me. It's a dot matrix miracle, a word-processing Turin shroud.

Jane's favourite story is about Pope John Paul II's visit to Scotland in 1982. 'Oh His Holiness,' she starts, 'I saw him. There were millions of us in that park in Glasgow. Oh, Damian.' She gets faraway eyes.

When the Pope visited, Granny Mac bleached all her net curtains and had the living room repainted, including the gloss work, 'just in case'. My mum took us all to a special Mass at the Grotto because Glasgow was so far and my dad stayed at home and changed the car oil. Everybody was waving paper flags of green, white and gold. There might even have been Majorettes. On the news we watched a funny-looking ice-cream van with a wee man waving. His fingers were dripping with rings and everybody crossed themselves as he rolled past and my mum sat in our living room moving her lips. Maybe the Pope can make her better.

When Jane shuts the shop at 5.30 p.m. she lets me turn the sign to *CLOSED* and we walk out together. Parked next to the shop is her wee black Ford Fiesta. She always offers me a lift even though I'm just down the road in the flats. But I can't let Logan see her drop me off – I've told him Scripture Union is every day now and he believes me. She stands with the driver's door open like she's waiting for me to say something and I just shake my head no thank you. I resist the urge to run after her as I wave her away, tyres crunching across the gravel, before walking down the road. St Jude is in my pocket.

Amen.

7

'I am . . . very much aware of the importance of Ravenscraig to Scotland, to Scottish jobs. In a way, it is more than to Scottish jobs; it is to Scottish morale. I know that. There is a Scottish dimension as well as a steel dimension.

I will not forget what Ravenscraig did and the way it stood and the way it carried on during the coal miners' strike . . .'

Margaret Thatcher, interview for Scottish TV,

4 September 1986

'WE'RE LEAVIN'.'
It's midnight. A million mirrored shards of Logan litter the floor, all of them staring at us. I hold Teenie back in the doorway – any further and she'll slash her feet. Baby Billy is bawling in his cot.

'Get yer coats and shoes,' says my mum calmly, her back to us. She steps over Logan to get to her baby, red and silver slivers sliding and cracking under her feet.

* * *

Mark Ellison changes my life just before the summer holiday at the end of Primary Five. He joins Keir Hardie Memorial

Primary School at the end of term, his Jason Donovan hair-cut neat and new when we're all ready for a shear. There's usually a space next to me so that's where he sits. My report card states, 'Damian has met his match this school year.'

After five minutes we find out we're the same age, almost to the day. We're summer babies, which makes us the youngest in our year. Our parents went to school together, leaving as soon as they were sixteen, then marrying and splitting at about the same time. Dads don't get custody so Mark went to stay down south with his mum and her fancy man but she sent him back. 'Her loss,' he says, flicking his fringe out his eyes with a jerk of his head.

My gain.

Mark is the fastest runner in the whole school. He's Sebastian Coe and Steve Ovett, his arms and legs a cartoon blur as he passes the finishing line with enough time to laugh at the stragglers, me included. And he's funny like me. 'You'll cut yourselves with those tongues of yours,' warns Mrs Rayson as we're told off for giggling.

For the final two years at Keir Hardie Memorial Primary School we must all endure BAGA – British Amateur Gymnastics Association – exams. Mark is the only boy to attain Level One. He flick-flacks across the gym, which once felt huge but now feels wee, and walks back on his hands pulling faces the whole time. It's like he's made of the elastic bands the girls tie together and stretch between their legs to play their complicated games. I never get past Level Five – the forward roll. I'm not naturally clumsy but I've learnt to be. No one expects the lanky asthmatic jessy to be athletic and I don't disappoint, tripping over mats and nearly hanging myself on the ropes. This way no one asks questions about the bruises and black eyes. Once Mr Baker kept me back and asked if everything was all right at home and I was going to tell him everything but I panicked and told him a long, lovely lie about going fishing with my dad.

From day one everybody loves Mark – boys want him on their team, girls want to comb his blond curtains. Nobody gets why he's my pal. Not even me. He's clever and pretty and cheeky and the teachers love him too. He dazzles with his front crawl when we start swimming lessons at the Council 'ool (*There is no p in our 'ool, please keep it that way*, warns the sign on the way in). The lengthy rules also forbid 'heavy petting' and we snigger at the smoochy illustration. Only Mark dares to dive from the high board twelve feet up. He climbs the ladder up and up then down into the deep end he drops, again and again. I close my eyes as he bullets through the surface making billions of tiny bubbles. Behind his goggles his eyes are open. He is without fear. It's like he doesn't care.

Me and Brian Southlands are the last two learners left at the shallow end. Even spazzy Leeanne Smith and fatty Moira Gardner have mastered the required single width of breast-stroke. They're all down the deep end throwing their arm-bands at us making chicken noises so I attempt a Mark-style dive from the side. Right on top of Brian. A klaxon sounds but we don't hear it and red-shorted lifeguards fish us out with long-handled nets and I wish the mouth-to-mouth would go on for ever. When I wake up I see Mark looking anxiously at me.

Within weeks we discover heavy petting. It's like what I did down the Sippy with Kev only Mark admits he enjoys it too and doesn't put me in a headlock after. Primary Five is soon over and summer is here. For the first time since my mum and dad divorced I'm excited about the holidays. I've got a pal.

Mark stays with his dad, Big Mark, who's only about five foot eight, in the Gas Scheme two minutes from my dad. Big Mark's live-in girlfriend is Tracey who we hate. Her ankles are as thick as her knees and we call her 'Grotbags' because she's such a big fat witch. She makes Mark do all her chores – washing dishes, hoovering up, cutting the grass. I help him so we can get away faster. We hate Grotbags more than Mary the Canary because at least Mary's good-looking, though she's not as fancy as she was. Her blonde curls have brown roots these days and I've yet to see her put a washing through that brand-new automatic machine. There's no lasagne now. It's like she's bored of being nice to me and Teenie. We call them 'the hoors'. We don't talk about Logan.

We can't go to Mark's cos Grotbags is always bursting into his room like she suspects something. The Bing is off-limits because they're building a big new estate of what Granny Mac calls 'bought hooses' there, promising 'two-, three- and four-bedroom family luxury from Brosley Homes'. The shimmering black mountains are being flattened by yellow JCBs, perhaps the same ones that made them, and the massive pond is being drained. I imagine the frogs coming back year after year looking for the place they were spawned. We could brave the Sippy but we don't know who'll be there. In desperation we sneak into Joseph's cave at the Grotto and start to kiss but it's like we're being watched. Mark says he doesn't care about Jesus. He's thrillingly Godless and says he knows there's no afterlife and I wonder how he can be so sure. He doesn't believe that Mary was a virgin either. I cross my fingers and hope he won't burn in hell. I decide to pray for him then get on my knees anyway.

We need to find somewhere else, a place where nobody will find us. Then it clicks: the Craig.

'Craig Under Threat!' screams the *Daily Record*. The *Motherwell Times* mounts a campaign to 'Save the Craig'. On the increasingly rare occasions he makes his custody week-ends it's all my dad talks about. They all blame Maggie like she's personally going to come and flick a big switch to *OFF*. I don't think she will. I don't think she's as bad as they say and if she knew how hard my dad worked she'd keep it open for ever. At school we sign petitions and write letters to our local MP. 'They can't put all those men out a job,' says Jane in the gift shop at the Grotto. I feel guilty about not visiting her so much but I've got Mark now. My dad says the Craig makes more steel than any other plant in the world so it will never shut. We will always have two sunsets, maybe if Maggie saw them? If it did close I wouldn't have to worry about my dad any more – a boy at school told me his uncle pulled a man with no legs left out the furnace and he kept burning away even in the hospital until there was nothing left to bury but his screaming mouth. Better to be pushed under.

The Craig is a futuristic machine-city: an orderly Mad Max. Dozens of factories serviced by thousands of men (the only women here dish out dinner in the canteen and they always give my dad extra). Giant cooling towers puff away together like old biddies at a bus stop. Centipede vehicles built with just one purpose carry tons of this or crush tons of that. Here and there are great mountains of raw material – ore and coal. White sparks dance from rivers of molten metal. Dwarfed by machinery, the men scuttle about in bright orange hard hats – white for the gaffers. Stretching into the sky, spaghetti stacks breathe green and orange fire. Everybody and everything is rusty brown–black. Only the girders leave here gleaming. Steelopolis.

The Craig borders the whole south side of Carfin. To get in you just cross the road at the back of the swing-park behind the flats and probe the chain-link fence until you find a gap – probably the same one used by a workman who can't be bothered to walk the mile down the road to the official gate with its barriers and security booth. Most men walk, swinging their sandwiches in a plastic bag from the Asda that took over the Fine Fayre, white on the way in, black on the way out. Granny Mac still mourns the Fine Fayre with its superior fish counter, good for a Friday. 'It's a right dear hole, that Asda, a scandal! They'd have the blood out your veins!' Pure black affronted, so she was.

In the first week of the holidays me and Mark find a gap and slip through sucking our ribs so we don't get caught on the wire. Straight ahead falls a break-neck slope of scree that makes the Bing look like an anthill. Mark has brought his schoolbag which he tosses down. It bounces heavily which tells us we'll only fall if we try climbing. So we slip-and-slide down on our arses, landing so hard I finally do a forward roll. Thousands of men work here but they're all spread out and there are plenty of places to hide. If we do get caught I'll demand to be taken to my dad. All the buildings, from the smallest shed to the hugest warehouse, are unlocked. Mark pulls at a door five times his height and squeezes in through the crack. I follow. Somewhere in the massive darkness a transformer whirr-crunks awake, thumping louder and louder till we run out, fingers in ears!

In a cosy shed with a kettle and some chipped cups on a dainty mug tree we find luminous orange hazard-vests that are too big for us. We put them on anyway. They smell of tobacco and oil and man. We toss stones into an eerily round pond glistening with black rainbows so soupy it takes a second to swallow knowing they will never reach the bottom. We imagine the Lady of the Lake raising an oil-streaked sword in a dripping black fist. We stop to share a can of Irn-Bru that Mark stole from his dad's and we imagine it makes us stronger even though we know it's not really made from girders. Maybe I'm related to the Barrs who brew it? Maybe I'm really a rich orphan?

We balance on big steel barrels and finish the can. Mark crushes it with his foot and feeds it to the pond but it just sits there. Somehow he's managed to smuggle new horror books out of Newarthill Library – our Junior Green Cards don't permit Stephen King, James Herbert or Dean Koontz. But here they all are. I'd never dare but Mark would. We take turns reading out loud. Particularly gory bits get read at least twice. Pennywise the Clown smiles his big red gash and boils our blood for candyfloss. Cujo is off the leash. Red-eyed rats swarm round our feet, their filthy fur tickling our ankles before they shred our shins. We open a practical-looking book by someone called Aleister Crowley that Mark says he got for 5p at the chapel jumble sale. It's full of swearing and makes little sense but we piece together some spells to kill Grotbags and Logan. We hold hands and utter the incantations, hoping for the worst. Then we hang upside down from a beam and pretend to be vampires from *Salem's Lot*. Mark kiss-bites my neck then we run around screaming. No one can hear us.

When we've scared ourselves stupid we do sci-fi. We are gripped by *V: The Mini Series*, which is like *Dynasty* but with bigger shoulder pads and badder baddies and spaceships (not counting the stupid flying saucer that abducted Fallon Colby).

We run round schn-schning laser noises and bicker over who gets to be Mike Donovan – the handsome journalist who reveals that the Visitors are really lizards beneath their human skin. Bright blue laser bolts miss us by millimetres and we take cover on a giant rubber conveyor belt that's easily sixty feet high but barely two feet wide. We run at it and clamber up on all fours, single file, up and up, and it's bouncing beneath us and a Visitor grabs at my ankle and we can't look down or we'll fall and die. There's no safety barrier, there aren't even any sides. Mark slides back and I catch his feet. We've got to go higher! They're gaining! Rubber slips and squeaks on our black plimsolls. Finally we reach the top and sit panting on a platform. From here we can see the whole world and somehow we've shaken them off. Up was a scary and exhausting half-hour. Down is a terrifyingly fast sixty seconds as we slip and slide and finally fly off the bottom.

Tired, we find a low steel bin and sardine ourselves in the conversion chamber from the alien Mothership.

'Maybe it'll make us normal,' I say and we judder like we're being electrocuted and secretly hope it will.

Maybe alien technology could make my mum better, heal her broken head. Then Mark steps outside and I'm Bea in solitary confinement in *Prisoner Cell Block H*. Because the whole place is floodlit and it's summer we don't really notice it getting late. Mark checks his watch. It's nearly seven. We were supposed to be home an hour ago. We sprint to the scree slope but it takes longer to climb up than slide down. We cross the road, looking both ways, and run back to the flats. Mark asks if I want him to come in and I say it's better if I go alone because I just need to get it over with. I look like I've done a shift at the Craig but there's nothing I can do now.

Mark runs home and I miss him already. I trail round to the front door, and down one side of the steps there's a smooth curvy handrail that wasn't there this morning. Logan isn't standing at the scullery window. I brace myself for him in the hall but he's not there either.

There are voices behind the living-room door but it's not the telly. It sounds like . . . I open the door and it is . . . it's my mum!

She doesn't get up, doesn't get a chance, I fly to her and Auntie Louisa is saying, 'Careful, son, watch yer mammy, mind, c'mon.'

My mum lifts the fag she's smoking so it doesn't burn me. My arms are Velcroed round her neck and I'm crying and her eyes are bluer and her face looks saggy and she's looking at me like I looked at the handrail. Like I'm new.

Overnight 1 Magdalene Drive changes. My mum is back. She's not the same but that's OK. She's wobbly on her feet and sometimes uses a stick. She forgets the names of things, like the kettle, and I have to dial phone numbers for her then remind her who she's talking to. We've all got to be patient and careful and help her as much as we can. Big Brenda still gets us ready in the morning cos my mum needs her sleep and we've not to make any noise after 7 p.m.

Auntie Louisa comes in to give my mum a bath. 'She's had enough nurses,' she says, testing the water for her sister as she would for Baby Billy.

I'm allowed to stay when Doctor Khan makes his weekly call. I stare at his hands and wonder how his palms are so white when the rest of him is so dark. I'm surprised by the coolness of the stethoscope. 'He'll be a doctor one day,' says my mum but questioningly not confidently. In a rare moment of girliness Teenie brushes my mum's hair and she winces with every brushstroke but doesn't stop her.

Logan all but vanishes. He hasn't lifted a hand to me since my mum returned. Now he's always at his mother's, cleaning out the dookit, or taking his pigeons to faraway places in big wicker baskets to set them free so they can race home. He times their progress on a special clock with a brass face and extra numbers that sits in a polished wooden box. I consider pigeon time. When he is home he's all smiles but they're his smiles. My mum and Baby Billy are both shaky on their feet, learning to walk.

My mum is keen to catch up, wants to meet my new pal, so Mark's allowed to come to the flat for Irn-Bru and crisps. My mum has forgotten she was at school with his mum but we fill in the blanks and she tuts about the fancy man down south.

One Sunday, just after my tenth birthday, I tempt my mum to the Grotto to meet Jane, who I've told her all about. 'Jane says yer a miracle. She prayed for you.'

Auntie Louisa is phoned and arrives and we all set off together. We're not far away when I notice bunting and trestle tables and people dressed too colourfully for Mass.

'Ooh!' says my mum, remembering. 'It's the Holy Ghost Fathers' Garden Fête!'

I nod and smile like I'd planned it.

'Ye know yer mammy loves a jumble sale,' she says, reaching for her purse.

'Ah'll count the money,' says Auntie Louisa, smiling and putting her hand out.

My mum lets her take it. Slowly, slowly we shuffle there. I want to run ahead but I stay on one side of my mum and

Auntie Louisa stays on the other. It's so warm the tarmac is a bit melty and my mum's walking stick leaves tiny prints. I wish for an ice pole.

My mum's not been out much so loads of people are seeing her for the first time. They come over. 'Och, Lynn, it's great tae see you out and about, hen,' they all say. 'Yer lookin' well,' they lie. They tilt their heads like someone's died. They talk louder than they need to and I feel angry. She's not stupid. She's just not well. They stare at her – this wee woman from Newarthill who survived a cerebral haemorrhage, the same thing that killed her younger brother a decade ago. Did you not hear? When she doesn't recognise them – any of them – they pat their chests and say slowly, 'It's me, Lynn,' then explain exactly how they know each other and how their mothers go to chapel together and on it goes. There's more than one person she wouldn't have stopped for normally. We've not even looked at the stalls, never mind found Jane, and we're already tired.

'C'mon, Lynn, time for a wee cuppa and a strawberry tart.'

Auntie Louisa leads us to the purvey where tiny old ladies guard giant teapots. As we sit in the sun with all the saints around us, everything feels OK. Then I spot Mary the Canary wafting towards us through the crowds. Auntie Louisa follows my gaze and nearly spits out her tea. Mary and my mum have only met in gossip. Pastry crumbs stick to the inside of my mouth. My mum smiles at me then looks over my shoulder. I don't need to turn to know that Mary's there. I can smell her – lipstick and Elnett and got-it-all.

'Damy,' she says, surprised. I flinch at the overfamiliarity. My mum's smile slips off her face.

'You've a cheek, Rosemary Murray, standing there like butter wouldn't melt,' hisses Auntie Louisa, not loud enough to draw attention. 'And this a house of God.'

At 'Rosemary' my mum's smile returns.

'That's enough, Louisa.' She shooshes her wee sister and inclines her head to Mary, pointing apologetically at her legs which look painfully thin even in the child-sized jeans she's wearing.

'Ah cannae get up, hen.'

Mary nods. No doubt thinking how innocent and pleasing she looks in a pleated yellow chiffon two-piece, she floats round the table and leans towards my mum. Ever dainty, she tucks her curls behind her ear. Waiting for my mum to speak, she leans closer. Louisa tuts at the unholy cleavage.

My mum is smiling now, really smiling. 'Hoor!' she shouts.

Mary looks puzzled. Her frosted fuchsia mouth falls open. My mum's hand shoots out and slaps it closed. I didn't know she could move that fast any more. Mary is stiller than her Virgin namesake for a second then turns round and walks away without a word, struggling on the gravel in her heels. Black affronted, as Granny Mac would say. Everybody saw but everybody knows Lynn Barr is in the right so nobody says a word.

'Have ye got a serviette, Louisa, hen? Ma hand's awful dirty.'

This is the highlight of the summer my mum comes home. Now she's back my dad pays us more attention. He makes every custody weekend and talks to her when he picks us up and drops us off and me and Teenie think this means they'll get back together. Mary probably didn't tell my dad about the slap and I won't grass but he knows. Everybody knows.

They're less lovey-dovey and he makes her practise her singing upstairs. I notice my dad's work shirts aren't ironed. She grates her own feet now. Sometimes she smells of Lambrusco. We don't get smiles any more. I consider telling my dad where she hides her bottles then I remember that Polaroid of me with all the make-up on and keep quiet. Another secret.

Baby Billy is walking now and mum has got rid of her stick. The first day of Primary Six she comes with me all the way to the gates at Keir Hardie without it. Me and Teenie grab a hand each in case she disappears. Every day we rush home expecting her to be gone again but there she is. My mum enters Baby Billy and his blond curls and big blue eyes in a bonny baby competition and Granny Mac calls it vanity. Logan spends more and more time at his pigeon dookit. The first term of Primary Six flies by and nothing bad happens.

Star Wars is the only game to play now. Me and Mark take turns being Luke Skywalker and rename his stepmum Jabba. Mark hopes for a light sabre at Christmas. I make it very clear I need a Millennium Falcon. The one bonus of divorce is two Christmases, two lots of presents from guilty parents. Add to this my mum's guilt about being away in the hospital and you're talking a Millennium Falcon with an *en suite* and staff. Me and Teenie save up the pocket money we get from our dad and go with Auntie Louisa to the Cooperative in Mother-well and buy my mum a bottle of Opium. We sneak a sniff and it's nothing like the perfume I made her with the Browns' roses in a jam-jar but we hope she'll like it anyway.

The calendar from the New Lotus Chinese Takeaway that hangs by the phone finally gives up Christmas Eve.

Me and Teenie are 'up to high do' on sugar because Mum let us raid our selection boxes but we've got to go to bed now or Santa won't come. I know fine well Santa has nothing to do with it but Teenie doesn't so I play along.

'Ah'm away tae Glasgow tae help Mr Claus,' she explains. 'He's got some big parcels tae deliver. But he'll not come if yous are bad!'

Teenie jiggles. She's asked for a horse (again). 'Not a My Little Pony.' We let ourselves be tucked in. It's not even four o'clock.

'Will Big Brenda look after us when yer out?' I ask.

'Och no,' she says. 'Logan's here.'

I force my face to stay the same until she's shut the door.

I must have fallen asleep reading with the light on because I wake up when it snaps off. My bedroom door is shut and there's not enough light coming through the curtain to see.

'Who's there?' I ask the room.

Silence.

'Who's there?' my voice goes. I know who's there.

'Who's there?' echoes back a twisted mewling girly me.

I pull the covers up over my head but they're ripped straight off. I screw my eyes closed. 'Ma mum –' I start but he belts me across the face with the back of his hand.

'Yer mammy nothin'. She's no here.'

'What for?' I ask. 'What have I done?'

'Nothing,' he says and belts me again. 'Shut it.' He clamps one hand over my mouth. 'Don't. Wake. Yer. Brother.'

With the other hand he pinches my left ear and pulls harder and squeezes tighter, rattling my head, and it's agony so I kick at him and as I do the lobe comes away from my head and there's warm wet relief as blood runs down my neck. He drops me on the bed and leaves a bloody hand on my pillow. All I can think is, 'These sheets are fresh for Christmas'.

'Gerrit cleaned.' He's silhouetted in a flash of light as he opens my bedroom door. 'Or no Santa Claus for you.'

I touch my hand to my ear and feel a draught in a strange place but it's still there and crusting already. I pat the sheets and feel stickiness everywhere. I don't know where to start. I fall back and everything goes black.

It's dark and my eyes are open.

'Damy, it's yer mum.'

I don't say a word. I make little noises and pretend to be asleep. She's got to go away. She can't see this. I've lied and lied to her and everybody else, told them all the stories they wanted to hear. She shakes me gently.

'Daaaaamy, guess what Mr Claus has brought.'

Plastic bags rustle at her feet. I can feel the Christmas cold she's brought in from outside. She's rattling a box, a big box.

'It's yer Millennium Falcon,' she whispers and clicks on the lamp to show me.

At light-speed she knows everything. The box slides to the floor. She leans over me and gasps and 'Oh's and touches my sticky scabbing ear and I can't stop myself wincing. She sees the bloody handprint on my pillow.

'Stay here.' She pushes herself up off the bed and walks out my room not stopping to close the door.

That's it. No shouting. No screaming. No nothing. Only the sleep-shattering smash of the full-length mirror.

'We're leavin'.'

8

'So I return to my main theme: building the healthy society. Many people are beginning to realise that if we are to sustain, let alone extend, the level and standards of care in the community, we must first try to put responsibility back where it belongs: with the family and with the people themselves.'

Margaret Thatcher, Speech to Social Services
Conference Dinner, Liverpool, 2 December 1976

'WE'VE NOWHERE ELSE TAE go,' my mum says, dragging Teenie with one hand and carrying Billy with the other. It's snowing. Everything is silent. We head down the brae towards Motherwell. Snow can't settle on the Craig – it's too hot and stands out dirty and noisy in a white muffled world. I hope we'll catch my dad on the road but it's after midnight and between shifts. There's a big banner made from bed sheets on gates saying *Save the Craig*. The *S* is backwards and I want to fix it. On the billboard across the road there's an advert for Shell that somebody's spray-painted with *FUCK YOU, MAGGIE!* Granny Mac always says if you've nothing nice to say, don't say anything at all. I wish Santa had brought Teenie a horse cos we'd all be sitting on it now. We've been walking for twenty minutes when a taxi finally stops and when my mum says 'Forgewood' the driver hesitates and I do too but we get in anyway. Forgy is always in the *Daily Record* – it's Europe's biggest housing estate, noted for stabbings, chip-pan fires and gangs. Even the 'polis' are scared of Forgy.

The whole block is in darkness when the taxi stops outside. The driver doesn't wait for us to be let in. 'Wit the fuck?' shouts a man's voice through the intercom by way of hello.

'Joe, it's me, Lynn,' my mum snaps at her younger brother.

We're buzzed straight up and Auntie Cat appears, belting up a pink housecoat and looking confused.

Uncle Joe stands square, bare-chested in a pair of green Gola shell-suit bottoms, ready for a fight. 'Wit the fuck?' He points at me, at my bloody ear.

Cat takes me and Teenie into the spare room and tucks us top to toe in a single bed then retreats to the scullery to make tea and ask questions. Billy, somehow, sleeps in my mum's lap.

Teenie is sleeping. I'm lying awake trying to listen. These sheets rustle every time I roll over and they stink of pish. An hour later mum checks on us.

'Yous all right?' A pause to light up. 'This won't help Cat's nerves.'

No wonder Cat's nervy, married to Joe. He's a big man – not just physically – at six foot with knotted arms so huge he struggles to find shirts when he's got to go to court. Everybody calls him 'Big Man'. In the queue for benefits at the post office everybody waves him to the front: 'On ye go, Big Man.' There's never any delay or disagreement and certainly not from Cat or his kids: Shawn, Aidan and Tricia. If you mess with one MacManus – Uncle Sean, Uncle Brendan,

Uncle Thomas, Uncle John, Auntie Louisa or my mum or any of my million cousins – you'll have the Big Man to answer to.

'We're only stayin' a wee while,' says my mum, tucking us in even tighter. 'We'll be all right here.' She'll have the couch when Uncle Joe is finished sitting and smoking.

Cat appears, wringing a dish towel. 'Cuppa tea, hen?' she asks and the light, a bare bulb, goes out.

The blankets are itchy wool and soon I'm wheezing. I'm in my pants cos we didn't have time to pack anything when we ran away from 1 Magdalene Drive. I walk into the living room and ask for a duvet. I catch Joe saying, 'Ah'll fuckin' kill him,' then he spots me and I think he'll stop swearing and maybe smile at his nephew but he doesn't. 'Whit yae up fur?' My mum and Cat spin round, owl-headed. 'In this house when yer down, ye stay down, got it? And ye dae as yer told.'

Another angry man.

Cat looks like she needs to say something but as usual my mum gets in first. 'Joe, the laddie's had enough.'

'Aye well,' he says as if maybe I have. 'Bed!'

I fall asleep thinking about all the presents back at 1 Magdalene Drive.

So now we live in a flat in Forgy with my uncle Joe, my auntie Cat and younger cousins Shawn, Aidan and Tricia. I'm ten and Teenie is five. 'It's only till the Council gives us a house,' promises my mum.

Keir Hardie Memorial Primary School is twenty minutes and 20p each way away on the Number 44 bus. It's not a school bus so my mum sits me and Teenie at the front before paying the driver our return fare and telling him to watch us.

Joe doesn't work but he's always doing something and Cat spends her time running after Shawn and Aidan and Tricia who do nothing. When she gets a spare minute she sits down with a cuppa and a Tunnock's Tea Cake. She tenderly undresses each biscuit, ensuring she doesn't crack the perfect chocolate dome beneath. Using the only fingernail she hasn't bitten to the quick she edges the red–and–silver wrapper off before smoothing it flat with the back of her hand. From a drawer in the scullery she conjures a shiny silver ball which must be heavier than it looks from the way she holds it. After she's eaten the biscuit and finished her tea she smooths the new wrapper on to the ball, writing-side down. The whole perfectly round, perfectly shiny thing represents hundreds of Tunnock's Tea Cakes. Thousands of stolen minutes.

My mum helps Cat with the housework and Cat praises us for being tidier than her lot, which only makes them hate us more. Tricia pulls Teenie's hair and Shawn hits Aidan then blames me. They've all got nits. Cat and my mum seem more relaxed when Joe's out doing whatever he does. They spend lots of time talking then stopping when one of us comes into the living room. Sometimes they'll pick up a Kay's catalogue and pretend to be shopping and I hope they don't notice it always opens at men's underwear. For a minute's peace they visit their pal Clare Buchan – Clare The Bear.

Clare the Bear's den is an identical flat across the road on the ground floor. Not a single room has carpet. Her scullery has thick paper sacks of potatoes by the stone and trays of eggs by the dozen. The washing pulley is always going up or down. From oldest to youngest her six weans are: Kerry-Marie, Michael, Alice, Johnny, Fallon (after her in *Dynasty*) and the baby everybody forgets. Their dad is the Wee Man

– half Clare's size, he lives in fear of her and 'works' with my Uncle Joe. Kerry-Marie is my age and everybody agrees she was an angel in her first-communion dress. All the rest are Trouble. Clare makes me call her Auntie Clare because the Wee Man's big brother, Terry, is married to my auntie Louisa. All three women agree Terry got the looks but that doesn't matter because apparently he's 'heavy-handed'.

Because I'm too big to play with weans and I'm terrified of all the boys my own age the three women let me sit behind the couch. Quietly I pretend to read while they talk. I'm on the last Hobbit book. I learn lots. I know that Clare 'slips a powder' in the Wee Man's Buckfast Tonic Wine when she wants some peace and he sleeps for days. I know that Cat's dad's got mouth cancer and his nose rotted off so it's hard for him to smoke. The nose-hole is covered in flesh-coloured Elastoplasts that suck and sag like bellows with every breath.

Logan makes a custody claim saying my mum is unfit and there's not sufficient room for Billy at Uncle Joe's. The court makes my mum send Billy to Logan's mum while they decide. I know that if it meant never seeing Logan again I'd probably let him have Billy – he's never hit his own son. I know giving him away would break my mum's heart and I'm at least ashamed for thinking it.

Forgy is a war zone. People call it Beirut. Smashed windows stare you down and burnt-out cars sit on bricks from crumbling balconies. The grass is green when it's not brown with pit bull shit and evil emeralds from broken Buckie bottles sparkle on the swing-park where the swings are wrapped noose-tight round and round the frames. Mrs Patel has a cage round her counter because refusal to give credit often offends. She gets called 'Paki' to her face now her customers are finding it hard to pay back their tick since their benefits got cut. My mum gets less disability benefit now but she's no less disabled – she's still having trouble with numbers and words and her headaches make her cry. Even though she's got nothing she still finds money to give to Clare or Cat, or anybody that needs it, or seems to. 'The shirt off her back,' Granny Mac says.

Now nobody uses the bin sheds, once the latest luxury, because you don't want to go in there in the dark so bin-bags stew in the communal closes. We're closer to the Craig so we can still see the sky glow but now it's only every other night. On the dark nights there's burgling. The Craig is being forced to wind down. The men are fighting it. My dad signs a petition that's delivered to 10 Downing Street by steelworkers from the Craig. He's in Maggie's hands now. She'll do the right thing, she will, I think she will.

Clare the Bear was sewn into her polar-white wedding dress and she doesn't care who knows it, which is lucky cos everybody does. Her boobs are even bigger than Mary the Canary's. They jiggle and brim and threaten to spill out and I'm shocked when she puts one in the mouth of the nameless baby because I've only seen that on the News, the poor starving black women in Ethiopia trying to feed their hollow babies, the ones my Granny Mac goes round the doors collecting for. Every time I see Clare she crushes me to her massive boobs and they smell sour but not in a bad way. I think she knows they don't work on me. When she's not shouting at her weans or screaming at the Wee Man or singing 'Danny Boy' in her surprisingly girlish voice, she's smiling and I know my mum is thinking she should fix that front tooth lost when a neighbour said something about her

Michael. They were right but that didn't stop Clare wading in. 'Ah left her without a name.' Her laugh whistles through the trophy gap. The women sit talking and drinking strong sweet tea from chipped mugs. When things are very bad, or very good, they sip super-strength Diamond White cider and think we don't notice the cackles. Whatever the mood, Cat is always the quietest.

Motherwell Council is Doing Something About Forgy because they say that's where all the problems come from. They're right. It's minging, a total dump. The only person at school that knows we're here is Mark and he won't tell anybody. Joe's phone's been cut off and the phone box is vandalised so I write Mark long letters about how much I hate it here and he writes me back about how much he hates his stepmum. I nip Teenie till she promises not to tell where we're living because things are bad enough.

I'm still too tall and my teeth have come in funny and I get headaches from reading which means I need specs but I refuse to deal with them as well. Teenie is popular – her hair has stayed blonde, not that she bothers with it, and she's pretty but not too pretty and she's great at sports. She's normal.

The massive scheme-wide renovation means double-glazing all the windows and putting central heating in all the flats. All the coal fires will be boarded up so there'll be no shame if your chimney's not smoking. A central work-store is built and armies of plumbers descend and I worry Logan is among them. Unbelievably Uncle Joe gets a job. As a security guard. On his first and only shift hundreds of yards of copper pipes just disappear. Afterwards the Wee Man is seen shaking hands with the scrap man. Everybody knows but nobody will grass him up – not here. Joe is clever enough not to get caught so he's probably clever enough for a proper job but I don't complain when there are new shoes and a new school uniform for fast-growing me.

From behind Clare the Bear's couch I hear more and more about a man called Dodger. It's party central here every Friday when the furniture is pushed to the wall and everybody sings to Daniel O'Donnell or some other pirate tape. I spotted Dodger dancing. He's shorter than Joe but taller than the Wee Man, his hair is thinning but what's left is black and I've never seen a tan like it. His teeth are white like my dad's but not false cos you can see his fillings when he laughs and his eyes are brown sugar. 'Half-caste,' cackles Clare and I know without looking her boobs are shaking. Dodger likes a drink, they all do, but he really does. My dad never drinks and Logan doesn't either, not really. My mum didn't drink till we had to move here – at first I thought it was her tablets making her stagger and slur. I beg her not to drink with them but she ignores me.

'Aw c'mon, Lynn,' says Cat. 'Let yer hair down.' They all laugh. Even Uncle Joe's got longer hair than her tight red curls.

So my mum starts off with a wee Diamond White. Dodger drinks till he bounces from foot to foot like a bandy lizard on hot sand. My mum dances with him and he makes her laugh. He's a good drunk, a happy drunk, till he's too drunk, then he spews his ring and cries and conks out. Sometimes I watch a dark patch bloom on his jeans as he pisses himself and still he doesn't wake. Or he gets fighty.

'The man's entitled tae a wee swallae,' says Clare. 'But he'd never lift his hand, not tae a wummin or a wean.' Like Uncle Joe, Dodger's not a bad man, not really. He's just badly behaved. That's what they say.

I've got no pals here. Really I've only got one pal any-where and that's Mark and he's up in Newarthill but not allowed to visit. I see him at school and when my dad picks us up for custody we hide in his shed and gorge on horror books. My dad hardly has us any more, which I don't under-stand cos he's less busy now they're cutting shifts at the Craig. I sit at Joe's living-room window every second Friday with my schoolbag packed watching for the red Ford Escort with the figure crouched over the steering wheel to come flying round the corner. 'He's busy with work,' Teenie says when he doesn't show. My mum looks angry. I want him to come just so I can shout at him.

One of those abandoned Fridays when everybody's over at Clare the Bear's and all the weans are in bed, I turn the telly on. Joe says no telly after 9. p.m. Once he caught me watching and locked it in the cupboard where they hide it when the TV licence van comes round with its twirling dish. He's not here now. I read *Salem's Lot* with Mark and the film is coming on and I know he's watching it too so I'm not alone even though he's in Newarthill. I watch as the picket-fence town is slowly taken over by vampires that no one wants to believe are real. A wee boy is back from the grave floating in his jammies at the bedroom window in a cloud of smoke and he's tap, tap, tapping at the glass. 'Please let me in, it's cold,' he begs and I'm thinking would I let Teenie or Billy in? By the end I'm so scared I can't even turn round so I crawl into bed with my eyes closed and lie there till they all come rolling back and Cat is shooshing but I can't hear my mum. Where is she? Dodger's tanned face floats before my eyes.

*   *   *

That week there's no money so me and Teenie have to walk the three miles each way to Keir Hardie. My mum takes a hand each and soon we're in Motherwell town centre where House of Fraser has closed down and been replaced by a What Every Woman Wants! Superstore with giant pink stars screaming *99P!* in the windows. It's undignified, like the day I turned up at Granny Mac's and saw her gigantic elasticated pants drying on the line.

Past the shops we power up Carfin brae past the Craig where the giant cooling towers puff less and less. Banners sag on the gates and here are the picket lines I've seen on the news. Dozens of men in identical yellow hats and navy donkey jackets: they look happier than they do on the telly. I look for my dad but my mum pulls us on and we all ignore 1 Magdalene Drive as we hurry past. The empty windows have been Windolened which means new tenants will move in soon. Teenie's legs struggle so I give her a piggy-back. We pass the Grotto and I want to go in and see Jane and explain where I've disappeared to but we've got no time. My mum's lips move like she's praying. We make it as the bell rings. Every day she walks us there and every day she's there at 3. p.m. to take us back and I don't think once about how hard it is for her to walk all that way. On the journey home, even though there's no money, we all stop at Onesti's Fish and Chips and somehow we're all given a bag to share and my mum smiles at Mr Onesti and we all say thank you. 'Ah worked here when I was a lassie,' she says and I'm shocked to learn she has a past.

Friday comes and my mum isn't there. Three o'clock stretches to four and me and Teenie wait at the gates and everybody else gets picked up and to stop people talking I walk us to the bus shelter. The Number 44 stops for us but we've not got the fare and I'm too ashamed to ask for tick. I think about taking Teenie down the hill to Dad's. It's only five minutes and his house will be warm and there will be things in the fridge but then he'll know my mum wasn't there. Mary the Canary will answer the door and sigh when she sees us and keep us on the top step and toss her hair over her shoulder and shout, 'Glenn, it's yer weans . . .' So I start walking us back to Forgewood.

As we pass the Grotto the gift shop is already closed. We ignore 1 Magdalene Drive and rush down the brae past the Craig, which shows no signs of lighting up tonight. It's getting dark and Teenie says she's hungry. I don't want anyone to stop us but really that's what I want more than anything. Someone to take us away. I go for the short cut through the golf course which leads into the back of Forgy. I've never done it but Joe uses it. He never said it went through a graveyard.

It's not dark but it's not light so we're still safe from vampires but there's no such thing as vampires and even if there is this graveyard is full of crucifix-shaped gravestones. In fact aren't all graveyards? You'd think Dracula would choose a less stressful place to sleep. We keep going through the glowing blue not-quite-day-not-quite-night. Teenie says we should go back but what does she know? So far there are no dead hands grabbing at our ankles from the graves or bat wings flapping round our heads. There's nothing and no one and it's quiet and I think we're going to be OK.

Then I see it. Teenie sees it too. We stop.

Something is lying on the ground a couple of graves away. I squint through the losing light. It's lying face down like it's trying to kiss the body in the coffin below through six feet of soil. I see no fangs, no cloak but I know monsters don't always look the part. Closer up, the body belongs to a man in blue jeans and denim jacket. He's about Dodger's age and height and he's not moving.

'Don't cry,' I shoosh Teenie.

'I'm not crying,' she says and she's not.

I realise I'm talking to myself. I take my rosary off and hold it out in front of me with the beads wrapped round my wrist and, brandishing the tiny plastic cross, I walk towards the body.

'Wait here,' I say. 'Guard my bag.' For once she does as she's told. 'I have faith,' I say out loud to any vampire listening because you've got to believe for the cross to work. I think of all the reasons why Jesus might not have faith in me. I need to pee. I turn round to check on Teenie whose outline I can still just about see.

Standing over him the first thing I see is money. Clutched in his fist is a bunch of tenners. Notes and coins spill from his pockets. His jeans are muddy where he fell and his zip is down and I feel my cock twinge. His hair is matted on one side and I see clumps of something in the curls. A bubble of something dark, blood – his own or someone else's – is frozen for ever on his lips. It's the black of Buckie spew. As I watch it and wonder whether to take some money and run, run, run away with Teenie, the bubble pops. Another forms and I realise he's breathing. Without thinking I kneel down and attempt to clear an airway like in *Casualty*. I slide my fingers in his open mouth – still no fangs, not yet. Stringy gobbets slip out and I gag. Teenie appears without asking and helps me roll him on his side. His undead limbs flop about and I think if we took just a few notes we could get the Number

44 for ever and as I think this his hand grabs the hem of my school trousers and I kick it off and scream and Teenie screams and I grab her hand and run and we mustn't fall because that's when they get you and we don't look back and we get to the road and Teenie shakes my hand away and we run the rest of the way. When we burst into the flat in Forgy there's nobody there to notice us missing. Over the road at Clare the Bear's 'Danny Boy' is belting out.

The next night is Saturday and Clare the Bear's Kerry-Marie is supposed to come and stay with Tricia. Kerry-Marie is going to be a nurse and I'm going to be a doctor, everybody says I've got the height for it. We do our homework together while Tricia waits to do the hair on her nearly bald Girl's World.

Cat is supposed to fetch Kerry-Marie from Clare's and walk her across the road. Tonight she forgets so Kerry-Marie rushes over on her own without looking and gets stuck in the middle of the road like Frogger not knowing which way to go. She bolts forwards and Cat runs to the window when she hears the tyres screaming and we're not allowed to look and then Cat's screaming all the way into the ambulance that comes after Kerry-Marie goes to the Southern General Hospital in Glasgow. Cat's ambulance goes the fastest.

My mum knows all about the Southern General – that's where she went after 'taking the haemorrhage' but she tells us no more about it, won't talk about that time. And look, here she is. All right she's not got back to her Mills & Boons and only she can read her message lists and her balance is off but it's all getting better and it doesn't, no matter what Logan's lawyers say, make her an unfit mother. If my mum can get better so can Kerry-Marie and for a while we all hope and pray. Granny Mac appears with medals from the Grotto.

Clare the Bear refuses to leave the hospital. Somehow she fits on a tiny single bed by Kerry-Marie. Hour after hour she waits and as she waits she brushes her daughter's grotesquely swollen head. After a month of this the Wee Man tries convincing her to go home for a rest so she batters him and the nurse who pulls her off says surely there's enough of your family in here. Clare collapses. Next day she wakes up in hospital and goes to Kerry-Marie's bed and brushes hair from eyes that are closed for ever and tells the doctors to take what they need. She says she knows it's not the Catholic thing to do but it's what Kerry-Marie would've wanted and her heart breaks at the past tense.

It's a good turnout, nods Granny Mac at the funeral. I take the day off school for my first funeral. It's weirdly exciting. Kerry-Marie is dead, I write it over and over in a jotter at school then rub it out. She's the first dead person I know and I think she would have made a good nurse. Everybody's here, the whole of Forgy and half of Newarthill. There's a special coach laid on at the graveyard gate. All the women are crying and the headstones are more expressive than the men. Kerry-Marie's brothers and sisters are as smart as they'll ever be. They're allowed to stand up front but I'm at the back with the other weans. I'm tall so I see it all. The Wee Man is trying to hold Clare up as she sags towards the grief-shaped hole in the ground. All the male relatives are given a cord each to lower the white coffin. Clare demands the first cord even though it's not a woman's place. 'Ah brought her into the world and I'll see her out,' she declares. Nobody disagrees. As the coffin goes deeper Clare cries louder and when it finally finds the bottom she's screaming, 'Ma lassie, ma wee lassie,' and the Wee Man clings to her arm and she shakes him off and the women surge to her side. Too late.

She's falling, falling into her daughter's grave, and everybody is just staring and the priest raises his eyes for help when Granny Mac grabs her from behind.

Silence. Nobody moves. Soil crumbles from the edge, pitter-pattering on the coffin. The priest orders everybody back. I know it's not funny but I have to I bite the inside of my mouth to stop laughing. Clare's stopped wailing. She's sobbing now or is she laughing?

'The mortification,' mutters Granny Mac syllable by syllable. She takes Clare's hand and leads her back to the bus and everybody starts clapping because what else can you do.

The one person missing from the funeral is Auntie Cat. She's locked in the loony bin, blaming herself. 'Her nerves,' my mum says, wincing.

Joe visits every day and my mum run the house for Shawn, Tricia, Aidan, Teenie and me. Billy is still being fought over so he's with Logan's mother. Joe gives my mum his half-empty double bed and takes the couch and I start seeing Dodger in the mornings and my mum gives me a look which says 'Don't ask'.

All through the last term of Primary Six, Joe seems to get smaller and quieter with every visit. My cousins wet the bed more, which means more washing for my mum. I start to feel sorry for them then stop myself because I've got enough to feel and anyway they smell.

It's summer when my mum gets a letter from the Council. She reads it slowly, moving her lips, and I resist the urge to read it faster first.

'We're top of the list!' she shouts. 'Top of the housin' list for a three-bedroom semi in the Coal Scheme in Newarthill with a front and back door – five minutes from yer dad and Granny Mac!' she adds, as if she needed to sell leaving Forgy.

'Enough room for us all, eh?' says Joe, but it's not really a question.

Carefully my mum folds the letter back in its envelope. 'Plenty, Joe, Plenty.'

The next week we're sent another letter and told to go and visit the house that's top of the list: 15 Rannoch Avenue, Newarthill.

We get off the bus just a stop after my dad's house and walk over to the house. It's perfect – five minutes from Keir Hardie Memorial Primary and ten minutes from Brannock High. My dad is down the road, Uncle Sean is round one corner, Great-Auntie Mary with the green eye and the blue eye is round another, Auntie Louisa is two roads away and Granny Mac looks down on us all from the hill by the chapel. Granpa Mac spends more time in the back garden with his tatties than with his children. People agitate him and he's got a bad heart so he's left to his veg.

We go in the gate and the blinds are closed and I think nobody's in and it's a joke and we'll be sent back, when the front door opens and a mascara-stained woman invites us in. In the middle of the living room in her coffin is the outgoing tenant, Mrs Geddes. The top half is open and the bottom closed with Sympathy cards and candles on top. We nod at her. The room is full of relatives of all ages. I've never seen a dead person. I'm sure I'm not allowed to touch but I sneak a finger along her cheek. It feels like a frozen Bernard Matthews Turkey Roast covered in Mary's make-up.

My mum smiles at the dead Mrs Geddes and chats with her daughter, who she went to school with.

'It's a lovely wee hoose,' the woman sobs. 'This is the only way ye'll get ma maw oot.' At that the candles go out and the cards topple softly. 'All right, Mother,' sighs the daughter, to thin air. 'Mind you, it's affa draughty.'

So the next week we all leave Forgy: Uncle Joe, Shawn, Tricia, Aidan, my mum, Teenie and me. And Dodger. 'He makes me happy,' says my mum, when she tells me. When they're not fighting he does.

We're just about settled. It's a snow-dome Monday just before Christmas and there's a ghost on the front steps of 15 Rannoch Avenue, Newarthill. I spot her through the Venetian blinds – I can tell it's a 'her' because she's wearing a nightie. She's got no shoes on. Do ghosts feel the cold? Not in Stephen King. But my ghost looks like she's shivering. She turns her head to the living-room window, sensing me watching because that's what ghosts do. The steel blind twangs into place as I fall back.

Caught.

Still wheezing from this weekend's asthma attack I sit among the red swirls on the living-room carpet and switch on my nebuliser, taking a few really deep hits of the steam which only makes me cough loudly.

Definitely caught.

I pick at the edge of the carpet where my mum Stanley-knifed it round the corner unit she bought from Kay's catalogue to 'free some carpet for a rug'. I try inhaling calmness. My chest tightens. I mute the telly which is showing *Return to Oz* less than two years after it was at the pictures, which means it's barely worth watching but it's on anyway because I hate every single person in this house – except my mum and maybe Teenie and Billy but he's hardly here – but I hate being on my own even more.

My ghost knocks the front door gently but firmly, like a doctor or teacher.

Peeking into the hall I see her face twisted by the maths-paper squares of security glass in the front door. Her head is impossibly wide and her Admiral Ackbar eyes point in different directions but somehow they're staring at me. The letterbox opens and five doll-white fingers reach in.

'Damian, son, open the door. It's your auntie Cat. Ah'm home.'

I've not seen Cat since we left Forgy. 'Carted off,' my mum says. 'No right. Up tae high-doh. A wee shame, so it is. Don't tell yer cousins.' Of course they know – everybody knows – that Cat went mad.

The not-a-ghost on the front step is pleading with me now. Her teeth are chittering. 'Damian, son, it's c-c-c-old.'

It's easy to unlock the door and let her in now I know she can't just float right through like something from *Salem's Lot*. I open the door and she steps into the hall wiping her non-existent shoes on the non-existent mat.

Her fringe is cut really high like she's a five-year-old who's been at the scissors and her nipples are tenting her nightie. I look away, ashamed for her. Her skin is white, almost green.

'D'you want a cup of tea, Auntie Cat?' I ask, as much to break the silence as anything.

'Aye, son,' she replies, looking through me. 'Cup o' tea would be lovely.'

Cat goes into the living room and I go into the scullery. Who should I tell about this unexpected visitor? My mum's at the shops in Motherwell with Big Letty from next door – they've become fast friends. Joe and Dodger will be humphing the bags back on the Number 44 unless it's their Big Monthly Mobility Day and they'll get a taxi. Granny Mac would know what to do but my mum's told me I'm not allowed to tell her a single thing that happens in this house. Of course, Granny Mac knows everything anyway and she'll hear about this soon enough. We've run out of milk but I put four sugars in because I remember Cat likes her tea sweet.

Cat is standing staring at the telly.

'Here's your tea, Auntie Cat.' I step towards her and she doesn't move.

'You always were that well-spoken,' she smiles.

I sit down with my cup and unmute the TV to hear how Dorothy is getting on in Oz.

'NOOOOOOOOOO! NO! NO! NO!' screams Cat, spinning round, clamping one hand over one ear and sloshing scalding tea with the other. She rushes at me, tea everywhere, and I dance away. She chases me round the living room.

'What? What is it?' I shout and she points at the telly and I turn round and aim the remote control and you'd think I was pointing a gun. She stops mid-stride, nightie see-through with tea, and her shoulders slacken as the telly mutes. Instantly she's calm.

'Thanks, son,' she says. 'I can hear them.'

'Who?' I ask, already not wanting to know the answer.

'Them,' she says, pointing at the screen.

'But the sound's off,' I explain, adopting the tone of a doctor delivering bad news on *Casualty*.

'Och no, son,' she says sadly, as if I just found my first pet goldfish floating upside down. 'Them,' she says, gesturing all around with both hands. 'What have you got to eat?'

I know without looking that the cupboards are bare – this house runs down to the last tatty. My mum went on benefits when she left Logan and the night before she gets her money from the post office I carefully fold out the foil butter wrapper and scrape it without ripping so I don't end up with shreds of foil on my toast. The last of the loaf is rubbed with the almost exhausted foil. A suggestion of butter. Like medieval witches, tea bags get ducked repeatedly and the milk carton is rinsed so your tea gets stronger and weaker. But it's Christmas so there are six Cadbury's Selection Boxes under the tree – one for each child. She's never been to this house. How did she find us? I wonder if she knows her husband and children live here now. What will happen if she sees them? We've all raided them, filleting our favourites, leaving only the Crunchie. We know we're only cheating ourselves and in the chaos of Christmas morning no one will notice. The only one truly untouched is Teenie's because she saved it. Reluctantly I open it for Auntie Cat who takes out a Marathon. She smiles for the first time and all her teeth are black.

'Are ye sure?' she asks as if I might take it away.

I nod and feel my face go red.

She nips into the scullery returning with cutlery and her Marathon on a plate. She sits with her back to me facing the now-dumb telly and with great precision slices the chocolate bar into bite-size morsels. Her elbows move like a violinist. She forks each bit into her mouth, chewing daintily, finishing one before starting the next with her mouth tightly closed. I think of Dodger and Joe slurping and burping and wish all adults had such fine manners. When the Marathon is over Cat dabs delicately at each corner of her mouth with the hem of her nightie.

'Thanks, son.' She eases her bones into the couch. 'That was lovely.' You'd think I'd fed her caviar.

I take her plate to the scullery and it's only when I put it in the sink that I notice the Marathon wrapper is missing. She's eaten it.

Cat's still hungry so I let her have the rest of Teenie's selection box. It's past lunchtime and everybody will be back soon. I wish I was at school even though it's the end of term and we won't be learning anything. I could be sitting with Mark speculating about who'll be next to grow pubes.

'Ah'm better now, son,' says Cat.

'That's nice,' I say.

'Och, loads better.' She taps her head. 'The doctors widnae have let me go if ah wisnae better, wid they? Is that not right? It's care in the community.'

I don't dare disagree. We sit and watch Dorothy on mute. There's no place like home.

9

'Yes, one is concerned but governments cannot prevent people from getting AIDS – but people can themselves, by the way in which they conduct their lives and that is what we are having to say to them: "Look! These are the dangers. These are where they arise. Now, if you do that, then you are liable to get AIDS!"'

Margaret Thatcher, radio interview for IRN,
January 1987

I CATCH AIDS IN 1987. I'm not sure exactly how but I've definitely caught it so I'm definitely going to die: horribly and soon.

I'm eleven.

'Act normal,' I tell myself as the advert that's been going round the playground finally comes on the telly. Our living room is full, as usual, with my mum and Dodger on the armchair and Joe, Shawn, Tricia and Aidan on the couch with me and Teenie on the floor in front of the telly. Billy's at Logan's again. Normal.

'There is now a danger that has become a threat to us all,' begins a plummy English voice that I vaguely know from something else. Something else embarrassing. On the screen an obviously papier mâché mountain explodes and I've seen better special effects on *Terrahawks*. 'It is a deadly disease and there is no known cure.' Joe shooshes Tricia who is crying because Aidan nipped her. Teenie would rather be outside playing but it's dark so she starts girning and I nip her which I never do and she's so shocked she actually shuts up.

'The virus can be passed during sexual intercourse,' and we all snigger and I join in even though I feel sick inside. More shooshing. This threatens to be as mortifying as the time these women with shaved heads invaded the News and Sue Lawley got all flustered and I asked what a lesbian was. On the telly a workman's hands chisel a word out of black stone and chapel bells ring doomily. 'Anyone can get it.' Anyone, yes, but. 'Man or woman. So far it has been confined to small groups. But it's spreading.'

I am in that small group, I know I am. I must have it already. I look at the cream rug I'm sitting on and see the AIDS spreading out from me like a stain. 'So protect yourself. Read this leaflet when it arrives. If you ignore AIDS it could be the death of you. So don't die of ignorance.' The workman's hands finish their work and the epitaph is complete: *AIDS*. I see my name on the tombstone as it falls towards the grave.

I go up to bed. I'm the only person at 15 Rannoch Avenue with their own room. My mum and Dodger sleep at the front over the living room. Teenie shares her room with Tricia and Shawn and Aidan and Billy when he's here. I've got the 'quiet' room at the back. 'So he can study,' my mum says when Teenie takes the huff, knowing she thinks homework is a kind of punishment. I've hammered nails into the wooden doorframe and bent them back to make a claw-like lock. Nobody gets in without my permission.

I lie awake late enough to hear Uncle Joe climb over the back fence to Big Letty next door who welcomes him in with her throaty smoker's laugh. We all know he does this most nights but we're not allowed to say a word. I don't know what happened between him and Cat that day. They came back from Motherwell and he turned whiter than her nightie when he saw her and I was sent upstairs and they both left soon after in a taxi. She lives with her mum and dad in Forgy now and we don't talk about it and that's that, God bless her.

Lying there I remember where I heard the man's voice on the telly. He was that old English 'poof', the Naked Civil Servant, the one my mum let us watch a little bit too long. How could he be so proud of what he was? Did he not know he was going to hell? At least in hell I won't have to worry about making sure Uncle Joe puts all the 50ps back in the gas meter. Until yesterday I was excited about our orientation visit to Brannock High School. Now I practise lying still for my coffin and stare at the ceiling thinking about the leaflet that's on its deadly way. I sit up and scribble plans for my funeral in the *Smash Hits* diary Mark got me for Christmas. Obviously my epitaph can't say what really killed me. So what will it say? Will I put my middle name on there? I hope to God I get what Granny Mac, who oversees all the wedding and funeral purveys and the meetings of Alcoholics Anonymous and anything else that happens in the chapel hall, calls a 'good turnout'. Not getting one is like dying a second death. 'Sad,' she says, plunging her meaty hands into boiling water to rinse the pale-green cups with *Beryl* stamped on the bottom. 'That's that.'

Cancer gets you the most sympathy. If somebody in the village gets it Granny Mac turns up on their doorstep, invited or not, offering a selection of blessed amulets from various saints. She whips open her Dannimac like a flasher and the lining is pinned with prayer cards and medals that promise to cure you if you just believe. She regularly stocks up at Carfin Grotto and sends them away to be prayed over by monks and nuns in Africa because they're cheaper. She knows everybody in Newarthill and everybody knows her. Their business is her business but she's not a gossip, oh no, she's just a concerned Catholic. You know you're in trouble if she presses St Jude into your palm.

The leaflet arrives the next morning along with the usual *FINAL FINAL* demands and the latest catalogue for Uncle Joe who orders goods he'll then sell at the pub and deny were ever delivered. A real entrepreneur. So here I am waiting by the letterbox. 15 Rannoch Avenue is bad enough without AIDS. I'm lucky I'm unpopular because Mark is the only pal I'd dare bring here. He stays every Friday night. We barricade my bedroom door and read the latest Stephen King. Lately we've been getting into fantasy too and we're working our way through *Gormenghast*. In all these worlds it's me and him against everybody else. Mark doesn't care that there's no vinyl on the concrete scullery floor that's silvered with slug trails every morning. I wish we had a dining table where everybody sat down for meals and talked. I'm mortified by our out-of-fashion Venetian blinds. The least I can do is stop AIDS coming into our house.

That Easter at church, or maybe chapel, I learned that the Jews painted their front doors with lamb's blood to make the plague pass over. I am the first-born son in this house. It's probably already too late for me but maybe I can spare the others, stop them catching it. Already I take my toothbrush to bed to stop anyone else using it by accident. Shaving is years away but if I make it there I'll hide my razor. Anyway, the only lamb I've ever eaten starts life frosty in the freezer so daubing the door with blood is a no-go.

Maggie says AIDS is a threat to national security. I scan the leaflet quickly: 'There is no cure. And it kills.' Granny Mac has no amulet for AIDS.

I stuff the leaflet in my schoolbag, sling it over my shoulder and run out the door just as my mum comes downstairs. As I run round the corner to the black steel gates of Keir Hardie Memorial Primary, I imagine her sobbing over my grave. It's a comforting thought. Maybe grief will bring her and my dad back together? I won't be there to see it but at least I'll get the credit. Because I'm a Primary Seven, even a geeky Primary Seven, the younger kids move out my way. I'm the tallest boy in the school.

As always Mark is easy to find: he's showing off at elastics with the girls. He's the only boy that plays. I don't get the appeal of knotting together hundreds of differently coloured elastic bands and stretching them between their shins to form a complex web that one of them jumps through while the others sing a stupid song. 'She is handsome, she is pretty, she is the girl from the golden city,' they chant as Mark nips between the tiny spaces, avoiding painful pings and getting faster and faster with the rhyme. He shoots me a look that says wait. They shout the last line: 'How many kisses did you get last night?' At that he leaps out the elastics to applause and runs over to me before any of the girls can claim their kisses. Amanda Ferguson looks gutted.

'Shhhsht,' he says. I spot an identical leaflet sticking out of his pocket.

'We've got IT,' I hiss, as if this will stop us getting IT. We sneak out the playground and sit on the quiet steps of the school clinic where we went for the bollock cough check-up, where I was worried I'd go hard when the doctor touched me.

'I know,' he shrugs, seemingly unbothered.

I can't believe this. We're dying and he doesn't care. Mark is brave enough to dive off the highest board at the swimming baths – he's the only pupil in the history of the whole school ever to do it. Without blinking he torpedoes the deep end and the bubbles in his tunnel of speed are beautiful. But this is taking bravery too far.

'What are we going to do?' I panic, jabbing at the leaflet so hard it rips.

'Die,' he says, laughing and skipping away.

'It's not funny,' I shout, running after him, careful to pocket the leaflet. 'I don't want to die. I want to go to Brannock and . . . and –'

'And what?' says Mark, pulling me close in a way that would look like a headlock to anybody walking round the corner.

Danny, Kev, Mark . . . all that carrying on in the dark. That's what will kill me, kill us all. 'Most people who have the virus don't even know it. They may look and feel completely well.' I feel fine, apart from asthma. But what about the spots I've started getting? The birthmark on my neck that everybody calls my love bite, has it changed, is it a lesion? I run my finger over it and feel tiny bumps. Were they there before? 'Those most at risk now are men who have anal sex with other men.' I know what an anus is, mainly from Tanya the Rottweiler, that belongs to Dodger's pal Andy. Her tail was docked too high so her brown-pink arsehole winks at everybody all the time. But what is 'anal sex'? Does a finger count, a tongue, an ill-advised Action Man? What exactly is 'seminal fluid'? Is this the mythical spunk that all the older boys brag about?

'Listen,' says Mark, trying to calm me down. 'If we've got it, we've got it and the leaflet says there's nothing we can do. There's no cure and that's that. We'll just have to die. But it says here it only affects adults. We're not adults yet, well you're not.'

Recently Mark sprouted pubes and we all saw in the changing rooms at the baths so now when the school grass gets cut we stuff our trousers full of cuttings and run round shouting 'BUSHY'. Mark was first, as always. The only activities I beat him in are academic and even then he's not far behind. When it comes to pubes I'm not first or second but definitely not last. Poor Stephen Thomson probably still gets called 'Baldy Balls'.

The bell rings and we go in. I notice some of the girls have been at their mums' make-up today mainly because the ones who haven't look younger than ever.

'You're ambassadors for Keir Hardie when you go over there,' warns Mr Baker, pointing out the window to Brannock High School which is just across the road but a world away and so new we can almost smell it. 'So best behaviour!'

The bad behaviour starts before we're out the playground. Somebody grabs my collar from behind and stuffs some paper down there. I don't need to read it to know what it is. 'AIDSY,' shouts Egg, running rings around me. Before he can repeat it Mr Baker lifts him up into the air, dropping him right by his side and he walks the rest of the way in nervous silence. Primary Seven has the stationery cupboard for solitary confinement. Who knows what punishments await at

Brannock High School? 'AIDSY,' someone else whispers. So I've got a new name to add to the others. Mark looks ahead to the new school: it's like he hasn't heard.

Weeks become months and suddenly we're in our last term at Keir Hardie Memorial Primary School. Soon we'll no longer be the big ones in a school of wee ones. Neither of us is dead yet but Mark has full-blown acne and we worry lots about that. Could his spots be a symptom? For a while we cease shenanigans but one Friday night we just can't stop ourselves. Might as well be hung for a sheep as a lamb, Granny Mac says.

Granny Mac gets all the papers on a Sunday which means the *Sunday Mail* AND the *News of the World* and spends hours tutting deliciously and pointing out especially filthy stories to my Granpa, who is only interested in football and horse-racing. The papers are forbidden to visiting grandchildren, of which there are at least twenty. One Sunday I am scrunching the Screws, as Auntie Louisa calls it, for kindling and read a story about Tom Jones being a sex addict who cleans his cock with Listerine to stop AIDS after all-night romps. Minutes later I'm in my granny's bathroom feeding my cock into her mouthwash. Aesop's clever crows and their pebbles, I think, as pink flesh displaces green liquid. It burns! Oh it stings like nothing else. I turn on the cold tap and splash my cock but it only makes it worse. Tom Jones must taste minty, I think as I top the mouthwash up with water and put the bottle back in the medicine cabinet.

Only when I'm brushing my teeth at home that night does it click that Granny and Granpa Mac must be doing the same.

I'm top of my class most years. When it's not me it's Brian

Southlands because he's better at maths and some years are more mathsy than others. Me and Brian are both tall and both come from broken homes. Only mine is more broken than his and when word goes round the village about the drinking and the dancing and the fighting and the dirty Venetian blinds Brian says his mum says he's to ignore me. She might be divorced but her house is no midden. I don't mind that much because I've got Mark.

All marks in all tests, except PE, are added up because we're all competing for the Dux medal. 'Dux comes from the Latin noun for "leader",' explains Mr Baker. The medal has my name on it as surely as the Superstars cup has Mark's. Based on the really boring telly show, Superstars demands sprinting, running round and round the football field, gymnastics and swimming and climaxes in an obstacle course rigged together in the school gym. Teenie has already decided she'll win it when she gets to Primary Seven and she probably will.

I feel everybody staring as the whistle goes for me to start the obstacle course. I learned to be clumsy long ago – after a while people stop asking what you did to yourself. Nobody watching now expects me to be able to snaglessly scrabble underneath the netting or successfully vault the horse and I don't disappoint, even throwing in a comedy fall that's more painful than I planned. Taking the high jump in one swoop of my long legs is the only accomplishment I allow myself. Mark aces every event, leaving even Egg standing.

We take more tests than usual for the Dux. Reading is all Mark and I do when we're not at school, well almost. We spend ages in Newarthill Library and enjoy it all the more because none of the boys who call us names ever come in there. Doesn't stop them hanging round outside to get us on the way in or out. When we both turn twelve our green junior library cards will finally turn yellow for adult and all the James Herbert and Stephen King books we sneak out now will legitimately be ours.

I come top of all the spelling and reading and writing tests. Brian is second or even third. Then it's maths. I never got the hang of decimals after missing that first day and I'm supposed to be practising. Fractions I could tackle but all this 0.25 non-sense is beyond me. The dots move like the ants Mark and I spent one summer day frying with the pebble lens from Granny Mac's reading specs.

Instead of doing maths, me and Mark master the mambo. As soon as *Dirty Dancing* comes out we swoon for Swayze, we want to put Baby in a corner so we can have him all to our-selves. The attitude! The hair! The hips! Mark and I take turns getting the video out of the shop, pretending it's for my sister. Nights we should have spent clicking at calculators and puzzling with protractors are dedicated to working out the exact steps. Pause, rewind, play. Pause, rewind, play. We bicker over who gets to be Johnny and who gets to be Baby and decide to take turns. Somehow along the way we accept we are, well, completely gay. We've both been called 'poof' enough to get the message.

'Actually I'm bi,' Mark insists, citing his deep love for Kylie off *Neighbours*. We found out about bisexuality when Freddie Mercury from Queen admitted he liked men and women in Granny Mac's *News of the World*. I say I'll try being bi too so we're both the same. Maybe being bi will make us less likely to get AIDS. All these worries are secondary to the need to get those dance steps down.

*　　*　　*

After acing his BAGA exams, Mark can do the bending backwards to touch his ankles with his head thing – a skill certain to be useful in later life. I can only watch and wince but I'm getting better, dropping my clumsy act and convincing my limbs they can actually coordinate. One day we decide to practise on the water pipe spanning the burn that runs through Newarthill and on through New Stevenson to Holytown and beyond. In places it's three feet deep and it's where Asda trolleys go to die.

OK, the pipe over the burn isn't a log over a river in America but, with no fear of the twenty-foot drop, Mark ignores the *Warning* sign and scissors his legs over the barbed wire, being careful not to catch his now hairy balls. I pass him the ghetto blaster containing the precious cassette and I don't look down as he helps me over. With great seriousness we take up our positions to re-enact the bit of the film I'm surprised we didn't wear out watching. In our thin elasticated plimsolls we grip the pipe, get our balance and then Mark clicks play and we dance and we dance. '1,2,3, 1,2,3,' Mark counts over and over and we repeat the lines of the film backwards and forwards till we are Johnny and Baby. We only snap out our Swayze haze when we notice we're not alone. Standing either side of the pipe are some boys. They're the same boys I made sure were never with me and Danny in the Wendy house at playschool. The ones who put me in that wardrobe and threw me off that cliff in the Bing. The ones who wait outside the library. They dance around bending over for one another, shouting 'POOF, PANSY, AIDSY' and, just for me, 'BARBIE'. Danny is one of them. He's laughing with the rest but, I convince myself, not quite as much.

The cassette stops with a click. The mambo is over. We're trapped.

Without speaking, Mark and I look at each other, grab the ghetto blaster and drop into the fast-flowing water. We scream at the cold and laugh as it carries us away sliding over rocks and dangerously close to a trolley and the boys shake their fists in frustration like baddies in the movies. Danny doesn't chase us. When they're well behind us we grab some grass and drag ourselves out, shaking with cold and fright. Watching out for them we run back to Mark's singing 'I've Had The Time Of My Life'.

So it's not surprising I still don't get the point of decimals. If only they tested us on the mambo. I put my pencil down after the final maths test and it's one of the last times I'll ever use a pencil because at Brannock you're allowed a pen.

Mark is crowned the Superstar of Primary Seven 1987 at a full assembly with the whole school crammed into the gym, ranked from wee Primary Ones at the front to us Primary Sevens at the back with the teachers sitting on the stage where we've all done the Nativity. As the Dux is announced I start to stand up and Brian Southlands does too. It's a mistake, surely. A joke, maybe. On stage Mark's acne flushes red for me. I am not the fastest or the coolest but my hand is always first up. Brian walks forward to receive his medal like Luke Skywalker at the end of *Star Wars*. It should be me. What have I got if I haven't got brains? Miss Carey, the head-mistress, pronounces Damian Leighton Barr as *proxime accessit*, Latin for 'he came nearest'. I almost forget to stand up. Mr Baker produces a Polaroid camera. FLASH! He captures my failure for ever. It spits out a square and slowly we all swim out of the grey nothingness. Mark with his Superstars cup, Brian with his Dux medal and me standing between them because I'm the tallest and blinking back tears. Mr Baker hands the photo to me with my runner-up certificate.

The bell rings and the day is over. The week is over. The term is over. Primary Seven is over. Keir Hardie Memorial Primary School is over. Parents wait at the gates and I push through their reunions back to 15 Rannoch Avenue with the Polaroid creasing in my hand. I tell myself it doesn't matter because AIDS will kill me soon anyway. Maybe then they'll give me the Dux out of sympathy.

That summer there's a general election and the evenings are hot with noise from the cars and vans that go round the schemes with their loudhailers. 'Vote Labour, for Scotland,' shout the reds from the back of a lorry filled with balloons and people wearing rosettes. 'Vote SNP, for Scotland,' shout the yellows from a packed Ford Transit. 'Vote Conservative, for Britain,' pleads an Edinburgh-sounding voice from the driver's seat of something big and new and shiny. He says Maggie is the best thing to happen to this country. She seems permanent and powerful, like the Queen. Who will we get if she goes? From the roof of Mark's shed we egg them all equally before throwing ourselves flat on the felt roof so they can't see us. Gritty bits sticks to our cheeks when we sit back up, sure we've got away with it.

Every hour tally vans go round the scheme selling sweets and things – Big Al is my favourite because he used to come to 25 Ardgour Place when my mum and dad were together and he always gives me extra chocolate sprinkles on my cone. He remembers me from before and ignores the gossip about the parties and fights at 15 Rannoch Avenue even though he knows everything about everybody because they all go to his big yellow van. *Be a Pal, Wait for Al!* is written across the back and two cones turn jauntily at the front. His big fat smile fills the serving hatch that he whacks aside with one big fat hand. 'Bonjoorno, Big Dame,' he always says and he won't serve you if you cut in front of me. He doesn't do tick but he does it on the fly for my mum so she can get fags and milk and tea bags and all the other non-ice-cream things from his van that must be a Tardis fitting in all that and him.

'Greensleeves' signals Big Al and when he's tinkled off to the next street we eat our ice cream on the shed roof and wait for the next candidate for Motherwell North to drive up. We can't vote but it doesn't matter who votes because Labour always wins. As pupils of Keir Hardie Memorial Primary School we were all walked hand-in-hand, two-by-two across the fields with the ghost mines underneath to see the small stone cottage where James Keir Hardie was born. I thought the hanging baskets out front were a bit fancy for the coal miner who became the first Labour MP. Mr Baker said they wouldn't have been there in 1856 and neither would the double glazing. A curtain twitched but nobody asked us in. It's a bought hoose! And whoever bought it wants none of us.

Loudhailers shout loads about saving the Craig and the economy and Europe but they don't say a single thing about AIDS. Mark and I scour the *Daily Record* for useful information and what we don't know we make up. Once we get bored egging them we go over and listen to what they've got to say and they all say the same things except the Conservative candidate who won't get out of his car.

They all give balloons out and we take as many as we can because we're planning a balloon shower in Mark's shed for our long-rehearsed *Dirty Dancing* finale. As I'm blowing them I realise I'm not as short on puff as I was, maybe my asthma is going away as I grow up. We're both light-headed and giddy by the time the last balloon is full. It'll be worth it when we do that final mambo.

Just before the end of summer Granny Mac turns up to take me to Motherwell for my new school uniform. She's the hand of God in this family and today she's wearing the brown woollen coat she keeps for trips to town. You can be sure my mum has the house spotless and all the bottles and cans cleared away and tea in the pot and a shop-bought cake that day. Granny Mac stays just long enough to point out that the Venetians are a disgrace before putting us both on the Number 44 to Motherwell. 'One and a half,' she instructs the driver, as if we're his only passengers.

The Cooperative is the biggest shop I've ever been in except for the House of Fraser where I got my foot trapped in the escalator. I was four or five in my blue wellies that I made my mum let me wear everywhere. She was shouting for help and banging the emergency stop button and my toes were getting warm and the stink of burning rubber was strong but I was just wondering what would happen when there was no welly left. I got TWO pairs of wellies from the white-faced manager.

'You'll grow into it,' says Granny Mac, pulling the sleeves of my blazer. It's the blue of the Tories who just won the election. Like everybody she says she hates Maggie but I think they'd get on, they're both used to getting what they want. You don't say no to Granny Mac. I imagine Maggie helping to pick out my crisp white school shirts. Maybe she'd show me how to knot my tie? She'd get 15 Rannoch Avenue in order, put Dodger and Joe out to work. The badge on my blazer has two clasped golden hands and the motto is 'Concordia'. The aeroplane? 'It's Latin for "harmony",' tuts Granny Mac. 'Do they teach you nothing at that Protestant School?' Everything is too big, even my black leather shoes, but I'm not complaining. All her other grandchildren will go from St Theresa's to Taylor High School so their uniforms are hand-me-downs. As her oldest grandchild my uniform is new even if I am a non-denominational disappointment. It smells new and I can't wait to show it off.

We go to the till and I'm worrying about how much it all costs when Granny Mac produces a book from her pocket and it's filled with stamps and she dares the woman to say something, anything. Burdened with bags, we stagger downstairs to the café and I am treated to a strawberry tart and we share a pot of tea and my Granny Mac blesses me with a rare smile.

'You're a cuckoo in the nest, Damian Leighton Barr, right enough,' she says, peering at me as if I'm already somewhere else. 'Whit's fur yae disnae go by ye.'

I'm terrified it will.

10

'I would say, let our children grow tall and some taller than others if they have the ability in them to do so. Because we must build a society in which each citizen can develop his full potential, both for his own benefit and for the community as a whole, a society in which originality, skill, energy and thrift are rewarded, in which we encourage rather than restrict the variety and richness of human nature.'

Margaret Thatcher, Speech to the Institute of
SocioEconomic Studies, 15 September 1975

FOR OUR FIRST DAY at Brannock High School me and Mark spike our hair identically using half the world's supply of electric-blue wet-look gel. 'Away ye go before ah start bubbling,' says my mum, brushing the shoulders of my new blazer. The sleeves have shrunk already. She's got to reach up to kiss me now. 'Yer daddy's double.'

I stop at my dad's on the way down to Mark's but Mary the Canary keeps me on the back doorstep. I've hardly seen him all summer. He's taking as many shifts as he can while the Craig's still going. Because we're now only five minutes away I often turn up after school but he's usually out. Sometimes I just look at the house and know he might be in there and that's enough. He never comes to our house and I'm glad because I'd be embarrassed. Whatever the weather Teenie waits at the top of his road watching for his car and he always stops for her even if it's just for a minute then drops her off at the bottom of our street.

'Mary, his car's right there,' I say, pointing to the Red Ford Escort with the black spoiler.

Her roots are really growing in now and what's still blonde is full of pink foam rollers all pointing at me like tiny bazookas. She's looking tired since my dad found her stash of Lambrusco bottles in her walk-in wardrobe. She's not hitting her high notes. She's wearing one of his work shirts, open, so you can see she's got no bra on. 'Hussy,' Granny Mac echoes.

'He's asleep,' she insists, loud enough to wake him if he was. 'Night shift.' She shuts the door in my face.

Nothing can bring me down today. I bounce over to Mark's. In a burst of paternal pride his dad snaps a Polaroid of us both on the top step. At the bottom of his street we join a dark blue shoal of boys and girls all on the way to their first day. Everybody looks nervous. We've heard rumours that first years get their heads flushed in the bogs. Mark has packed extra gel in his new Nike backpack just in case.

The foyer echoes with a hundred overexcited voices. We spot Amanda Ferguson and the boobs she grew over the summer. She's talking to some girls we don't know about who's the hottest on *Neighbours* – Charlene's Scott or Mike the mechanic. It's a universal language. We're impressed by her communication skills, reaching out to strangers. A quick scan confirms I'm still the tallest and I spot a teacher coming.

'Settle all down, first years,' she shouts. She looks younger than the teachers at Keir Hardie.

'I'm Miss Campbell,' she announces, smiling. Her hair appears to be two styles and colours at once – plum-purple spikes on top and a sleek black bob at the sides. The colours can't be natural and it's cool, way too cool for a teacher. We stare as one and she smiles at every single pupil.

Miss Campbell places one hand on her hip and giggles to herself, shaking her head. Her hair doesn't move. 'Right, first years. Settle down. Welcome to Brannock High School. You'll be having an induction assembly when the bell rings.'

At that the bell rings, louder and faster than at Keir Hardie, and I feel hundreds of people moving around with purpose. Turning on her heel, Miss Campbell leads us to the canteen where a hundred chairs wait around a lectern. Behind shutters the dinner ladies cackle and bang pots about. They go quiet when a hush sweeps in with the tweedy headmaster, Mr Margrave. He says he's very pleased to see us all but doesn't actually look at any of us, and he's sure we'll all do him proud and he has a voice you don't argue with. He looks like he plays golf and enjoys it. Me and Mark are busy sneaking looks at Miss Campbell sitting behind him. She sits smiling behind the headmaster like she's heard it all before. When he's done we all clap politely and Miss Campbell gets up. Did she just wink?

'Now, I'm going to read out a list of names. If you hear your name that means you're in Gibson House – my house. If you don't hear your name that means you are in Anderson House with Mr Galbraith who'll be along in a moment. Each house will then be divided into two classes.' She starts reading and soon gets to *B* for Barr! *C*, *D* then *E* for Ellison. And nothing. She's on *F* for Farrell, *G* for Graham. Mark squirms.

I panic. I can't do this without him. We've got to stick together. Separation is not in our plan.

I'm still taking this in when Miss Campbell puts her hand on my shoulder. 'Did you not hear? What's your name, son?'

'Damian Leighton Barr, miss.'

'Well come with me, Damian, you're in 1G2 – my class.'

And she leads me away from Mark, who is already tilting his dimpled chin up.

There are only five pupils from Keir Hardie Memorial Primary School in 1G2 and apart from me they're all remedial but we stay close for our first class – registration. Every day for the next six years Miss Campbell will mark us all on her register. Despite living only ten minutes away I'll be marked *LATE* almost every day. Staying up reading every night isn't good for punctuality. Neither are nightmares about the boy from *Salem's Lot*, about everybody being vampires and nobody believing you when you warn them.

After we've all said our names Miss Campbell sketches out the future for 1G2. For the next two years we'll take all our classes together. After that we'll be split into streams based on academic ability as we prepare for our Standard Grade Exams, what the English call GCSEs. So E1 will be for pupils on course for As and maybe Bs. E2 is Bs and Cs. E3 is everybody else. After Standard Grades the remedials will leave to go on benefits and we stay on for Highers, 'far superior to the English A level, giving you a broader base'. If you're not clever enough to sit Highers you take ScotVec modules in things like food hygiene. If you're really smart or really square, or both, you can stay on for sixth year for more Highers and something called Certificate of Sixth Year Studies (CSYS). Get an A in CSYS and go on to study that subject at a

Scottish university and they'll let you skip the first year. If I get As for everything I can finish uni and be a journalist like Mrs Hart by the time I'm twenty. 'Don't turn into wannae they yuppies, son,' my dad warned when I told him my plans.

'I will also be your guidance teacher,' explains Miss Campbell. 'That means you can come to me with any problems you have at school or home and talk in confidence and I will do whatever I can to help.' Pause. 'Bullying is not tolerated at Brannock High School.'

There is a special guidance room off the foyer with low, foam-filled armchairs designed to instil confidence and extract secrets. It would be easy to go in and sit down and confess everything but everybody in the foyer would see you. As soon as the door closes, rumours sweep the school: she's pregnant, he sniffs glue, her dad interferes with her, he's going to run away. Usually they're not wrong. So I decide to go on without guidance.

The rest of the morning flies by as we fiddle with high-lighter pens while we sketch out our timetables and work out where the different classrooms are on the map.

The bell rings for our fifteen-minute interval – we're too old for 'playtime' now. In the foyer I stand on tiptoe looking for Mark's blond spikes. Nobody's outside cos it's raining. The second years are the meanest, pulling at hair and spitting at us, maybe because they were us so recently. Third years and fourth years are more interested in each other but you've still got to be careful. We're completely beneath the notice of the occasional fifth and sixth years. Sharks don't eat minnows.

Or so I thought.

I've just found Mark and I'm asking him what 1A1 is like when I'm shoved from behind and fall on my knees.

Laughter all round. I get back up because I'm trying to make a new start and show them all I'm no poof.

'Barr?' grunts a tall boy with dark curly hair who has to be a fourth year at least.

'Yes,' I say, too formally, standing up straight and brushing down my blazer. I should have said 'Aye' and tried to deepen my voice.

Another big boy with nearly see-through skin and proper carrot hair sniggers next to him, picking his chapped lips. 'Me an' aw.' He grabs my shoulders and pushes me back down on to my knees on the shiny blue lino and hisses in my ear, 'Ah'm yer big cousin, Peter.' He leans right into my face. He has lovely teeth. Some older girls tell him to stop. 'Don't. Ever. Talk. Tae. Me. Got it?'

'Got it,' I nod. He spits on me before walking away. In the divorce I forgot my dad's two brothers and sister, my uncles and aunt. I can't even remember their names. We never go to see them. They never come to see us. There are no birthday cards or Christmas presents. Granny and Granpa Barr sometimes send a birthday card addressed to 'Master Barr'. Granny Barr is fat, even fatter than Clare the Bear. All she eats is cakes. When she's not scoffing she's talking and throwing her head back to cackle. She's always 'getting the glad eye' from some amorous neighbour. Granpa Barr is tall and thin and stooped and always looks surprised behind thick glasses. Like my dad he rarely speaks. When he does it's through Snowy – Snowy is their white Persian cat and whenever one dies it's instantly replaced by an identical feline with the same name. He'll say, 'Snowy, tell Mrs Barr I don't want mince for dinner.'

So I've been reminded I've got cousins with the same second name as me. They've not forgotten me. Well, Peter's not. Nothing to see here. The watchers move away and Mark helps me up but only after I put my hand out.

There's more indignity that first lunchtime. At the end of class, one or two of us are kept back. We don't know why until a list, which I read upside down, is produced from a drawer: *SPECIAL ASSISTANCE – FREE SCHOOL DINNERS*. I feel myself blush but my stomach growls gratefully. I find Mark and we queue up with our aeroplane-style trays and I get a baked potato with beans and grated cheese and a battered sausage and a vanilla slice with custard, all in their own portioned spaces. Baked potatoes are future food, something they'd eat in London. I've never had one. At the till I hand over my card and the dinner lady folds 'Monday' neatly and rips it off, dropping it in with the notes.

'Ignore them,' she says and only then do I click that it's me the queue is laughing at.

'Tink,' mutters one girl.

An older boy turns out his empty pockets and pretends to cry. My face is hotter than my lunch.

So far high school is not cool.

There's worse to come. Somehow the whole school has got a whiff of my gayness. 'Poof', they hiss in the foyer. 'AIDSY!' And they know I'm poor even though we're all in the same uniform. I think of Mary the Canary singing 'Coat Of Many Colours' and I know it's not true. I don't know how they all know so much about me. Most of them didn't go to Keir Hardie and half of them don't even live in Newarthill. I've not done anything gay. Have I? Do I smell poor? I don't smell like David Marsden – wet washing and potato peelings. For all her faults my mother is mad for bleach. She inherited this from Granny Mac who actually scrubbed chicken pox off one of my uncles with a wire brush. By the end of the first day I'm 'Barbie', 'Gay Barr' and the startlingly original 'Gaymian'. I deny it – to them and myself.

At 3.30 p.m. Mark and I meet outside as planned. Turns out 1A1 isn't much better than 1G2.

'Remedials,' Mark says. 'By the way, everybody knows you're bent.'

'They don't. I'm not.'

'You are.'

'I'm not!' Pause. 'So are you!'

We never argue. He turns left towards his dad's and I turn to go with him.

'No way,' he says. 'Not like you.'

'Not like me how?'

'I've been asked to smokers' corner,' he boasts, spitting. Since when did he spit?

Smokers' corner is basically a bin shed at the back of the canteen where you can buy a fag for 50p. The whole school knows about it and every now and then one of the teachers half-heartedly breaks it up.

'But you don't even smoke! You hate it when your dad smokes. If you smoke you won't be able to run the 100 metres or swim or anything!'

'Watch me,' he says as if he might have a pack of twenty in his back pocket right now.

I can't smoke. Our house is always hazy and choky. I nicked some cigarettes on a Wednesday when they wouldn't be missed – a few days later Dodger was scrounging in the ashtrays for extravagantly stubbed out fag-ends. I wheezed like one of the balloons I used to get from the ragman, the ones that always had holes in.

'I'm going,' says Mark. I put my hand out to stop him and he shakes it off. 'Get off me! Grow up!'

Mark isn't there to walk with me to school next day. He's on the other side of the foyer when I come in and turns his back when he sees me. We've got PE that morning and I'm thrilled and horrified to find the boys' changing room has no cubicles. Coat hooks line the brick wall and when I walk in wee Davie Fowler is dangling off one from his backpack. Andrew Frew, who's got taxi-door ears, is pointing and laughing. Fowler finally falls off. I take a hook near him but not near enough to be contaminated by him. Frew joins the other cool boys in the corner. They've all got pubes. The boys near me have fuzz if they're lucky. I sneak a peek when I can but they all just point and stare: 'maggot' is the worst slagging off and 'dong' is the highest praise. None of them is as hairy as Mark and I feel proud of him. We're all in navy-blue shorts and gold T-shirts by the time Mr Stewart the PE teacher jogs us out to the athletic field. The class before is finishing a 100-metre race and I see Mark cross the line first. Everybody cheers and Mr Stewart asks his time from another teacher and raises his eyebrows and joins in the clapping. Everybody loves Mark. Fowler stands next to me and I move away towards Mark. I smile at him. He strides right past.

After a week of not seeing each other all day every day it's like he's forgotten me. I turn up at his house on Saturday morning. For once his dad looks pleased to see me.

'He's oot,' he says. 'Playin' fitba.'

Football? Mark is playing football? Why? Who with? I've got the latest James Herbert, *The Fog*. We were supposed to go to the Craig and read out loud. Instead I run home and barricade myself in my room with my books.

As usual there's a party downstairs. When the noise reaches its predictable peak I shove bits of toilet paper in my ears and focus on the horror on the page. I imagine Dodger and Joe and all their drunken pals disappearing in the fog screaming then I realise I really can hear screaming. I unstuff my ears, pull back the nails from my door and head to the top of the stairs. Looking down I see a woman standing by the bathroom staring at the blood running down her lard-white legs from under her black-denim miniskirt. It's wee Sandra Gordon whose big sister Cora went mad with syphilis and threw a birdcage out the top floor of Carfin flats with a bird in cos she thought the whole thing would fly. Sandra is even shorter than my mum. She touches the blood and it drips off her fingers and she screams even louder. I'm halfway downstairs when a grinning Dodger bounces out the living room, dancing from foot to foot. He sees the blood but doesn't seem that bothered and shouts, 'LYNN!' There's a pause. 'LYNN-EEE!' he sing-songs idiotically and I wish he'd just go in and get her. My mum staggers out with a fag in her hand looking interrupted and sobers up in an instant shouting at me to phone 999. She locks herself in the bathroom with Sandra then Dodger tries to stop Andy with the smashed-in Goonies face, whose baby this was, from kicking the door in. When Tanya the Rottweiler starts barking and growling, I retreat to my room.

Monday morning and I head to Mark's to tell him about Sandra but he's gone on ahead again. I can't believe it.

That lunchtime I finally find him and he's too embarrassed to go with me while I get my free dinner so we agree to meet at the chippie. When no one's looking he gives me a chip and we walk and talk and it's all OK again. Coming towards us are two girls I know from 1G2. I recognise them as Heather Drummond and Sharon Johnson. They're both in frilly white ankle socks. All the other girls wear thick black tights. Mark is drinking a strawberry milkshake. 'Let's do a *Carrie*,' he says. It's one of our favourite books and we love the film. If I do this, things'll be back to how they were. He slugs half and hands me the cup, it's that thin plastic that splits if you grip hard. I walk towards the girls who look wary before they realise it's only that gay Damian Barr and he won't do anything and in that second I decide to prove them wrong. Direct hit. Pink milks runs down bare legs staining white socks.

'Periods!' Mark shouts. 'Yous've got yer periods!'

Sharon stands there dripping and bawling. Heather lowers her head and runs at me and I don't move and she kicks me once really hard right in the shin. I hop over to Mark who's pissing himself laughing with some boys from 1A1. They're all pointing and laughing at me and Heather and Sharon.

'Sorry,' I shout, my voice trailing off, not quite wanting the boys to hear.

Not stopping to dry her legs, Heather stomps back to school trailing Sharon. All afternoon I wait in fear, expecting to get in trouble, to be pulled out of class, but Heather doesn't grass. I try talking to her when the bell goes but she ignores me. So does Mark.

After a week of my saying sorry every time I see her, Heather finally shrugs. 'That Mark Ellison's a dick,' she says and I'm shocked to hear this girl with the Alice band swear.

'He's not, I, he . . .'

She looks at me, assessing my loyalty. 'Well, he is a bit.'

We start talking about *To Kill a Mockingbird*, which we're reading for English with Mrs Kennedy who we both agree is brilliant but mental.

I don't know how we become boyfriend and girlfriend but that's what everybody starts saying about us so that's what we become. They make smoochy noises at us in the foyer and dare us to kiss and sometimes we do. Valentine's cards are exchanged with *SWALK* and messages from *ANONYMOUS* even though we hand them to one another in person with a chaste peck and maybe a gift of a pack of Rolos. Our relationship is the Tooth Fairy, Easter Bunny and Santa Claus rolled into one but what does it matter so long as we both believe? Mark steers well clear and rumours spread about him and a slaggy fourth year. The whole school still says I'm gay but Heather defends me, even when I don't defend myself. If anyone gets too close she kicks their shins. Her nickname is 'Farmer Giles' because her family keep horses and she does look like a farmer's wife in waiting. She's the only girl in our year without a fringe and she never covers her pink cheeks with blusher or anything else. Hazel eyes unbothered by mascara hold your gaze. She's no slag. She doesn't care what anybody thinks or says about her.

Heather is a good person and good for me, I think. Maybe she can help me change. 'Fly wi the craws ye get shot wi the craws,' says Granny Mac, who approves of her family. We sit next to each other in registration, we cheer each other when we come in last in PE and we spend every evening together after school. It's not long until I've got out of sports for ever. Heather is less fortunate. I sit in the library longing for Holden Caulfield, watching the others doing cross-country in all weathers. Poor Heather slogs on through the rain catching everybody up, her boobs, two of the biggest in our year, bouncing in her sports bra. When the bell rings for the next class I use my laminated sick note – 'Please excuse Damian, he has asthma' – as a book mark.

Heather's house is at the top of Newarthill. It's one of the last in the village and the only 'bought hoose' I've ever been in. Her family used to own lots of land about here but sold it off so now it's just the farm and stables where her deaf angry granpa lives and the fields where her dad and her uncle have built bungalows. I thought only the Council built houses. Heather's parents both work – nobody works at 15 Rannoch Avenue but my mum keeps saying she'll get 'a wee job' when she's better. I keep nagging her to stop drinking and she just ignores me, tells me to mind my own business. Somehow she makes me feel uncool. We walk up the high street past the post office and Streaks Ahead Hairdresser's where I'll soon go for some ill-advised streaks.

Heather's bungalow has a red monoblock driveway and room for several cars. It's a palace. She lets us in with her own key. It's quiet. We've got the house to ourselves and I'm suddenly terrified she might think I should take advantage and give her a love bite or something but instead she offers me a drink and we down glass after glass of Irn-Bru while thumping our homework on to the dining table – dining table! I stroke it like my dad would a shiny new BMW. There's a microwave and Heather does us some chips in a box, which she gets from a fully stocked chest freezer. We watch *Neighbours* and Ramsay Street is just fading when her mum sighs through the door straight off the train from Glasgow where she programmes computers in a bank.

'Hello,' she says, surprised to see me, and Heather gives me a look. She's warned me her mum's English.

'Is your pal staying for dinner?' I enjoy the exoticness of her Cumbrian vowels.

Heather nods. I was never this welcome at Mark's. I introduce myself to Mrs Drummond.

'Call me Mrs D,' she says.

We follow her through to the scullery, which they call a kitchen, where a dish of precooked garlic chicken is produced from the fridge. I thought garlic only came on bread and only then on telly. Mrs D sets an extra place at the table. She will do this almost every school night for the next six years and she will never complain. Heather's brother wanders in. He's a fifth year with long hair tied back in a ponytail. He's going to do physics at the uni. Like Heather and her mum he's got ridiculously rosy cheeks. We're all talking about what we did today when the back door slams and in comes Heather's dad. Everybody sharpens up except me. I just keep talking. He is tall but would never stoop. His eyes vibrate in his head, they dance, daring you to watch them move.

'Who's this?' His beard is flecked with red.

Heather introduces me and her mum explains I'm staying for dinner. He asks my second name and I tell him.

'Big Glenn's laddie?'

'Yes,' I say, proud. He looks me up and down then shrugs. 'Tell yer daddy ah was askin' for him. Is he still at the Craig?'

I nod. He shrugs again, looks surprised.

'Well, tell him if he wants mair work tae gie me a wee buzz. Yer dad's good on the machines.' He turns his attention to Swarfega-ing the dirt on his hands into submission.

He knows that Maggie is going to close the Craig. We all do. Only my dad won't believe it and when I see his weary face I hate her as much he does, as much as everybody does. I feel stupid for trusting her, for thinking she would read his petition.

Dinner is eaten quietly around an actual table and I feel like I'm in a BBC One Saturday-night series. It's all so amazingly normal. Nobody shouts or lifts a hand. Dorny, the family dog, lies under the table waiting for crumbs. He's a black-and-white border collie, the only kind of dog Heather's dad would allow. We're actually excused from the table and scurry off to Heather's room where we close the solid pine door and flop on to her bed and burst out laughing before gossiping about everybody from school, what he said to her and she said about him and then we get our homework out and start that.

Heather's got one of the first portable CD players. It has a yellow sign on with a lightning bolt warning you not to look at the laser. She puts Madonna on low-volume and we hum along to 'Like A Virgin'. After an hour her dad throws open the door without knocking and we're both on the bed and he stares at the floor where I obviously should be and I'm flattered he thinks I'd be doing anything I shouldn't. He asks if I want a lift home at 9 p.m. and leaves before I can say anything.

Bang on 9 p.m. Mrs D sits me in the front of their G Reg Blue Vauxhall Cavalier. I buckle up and she smiles and we drive the five minutes down from the top of Newarthill. I try to make it clear I'm not bad for Heather by talking about school. We're about to turn into the top of Rannoch Avenue and I panic.

'Just here. Drop me just here and it'll save you turning.'

She brakes, saying that's considerate. I wave her away and when she's turned the corner I walk down the road and sure enough music is blaring out the wide-open front door and Dodger is punching the fuck out of some random in the front garden. I get closer and . . . it's my mum and I'm running running running but before I get to her she's up on her feet with a Buckie bottle in one hand and while Dodger's looking at me she smashes it round his head and he goes down, right down. She smiles at me and waves but I ignore her as I walk in the front door with my schoolbag over my shoulder.

When we have to pick our Standard Grade options Heather and me conspire to take the same subjects so we can spend all our time together. Everybody does English and maths. After that, it's up to you.

Neither of us picks music. I like it but I can't afford my own instrument as I learned when I had to borrow a communal recorder. They stand steeped in a jar of Milton's sterilising fluid to prevent the pupils sharing them from also sharing germs. Since AIDS, Mrs McKay, who wears a leather miniskirt with no knickers, refuses to dilute the Milton's and she won't let you rinse your recorder. She makes you play with the taste of Milton's in your mouth. All the boys take turns dropping pencils on the floor so they can get a look up her skirt. Even me. Somehow I get an A which means I'm invited to play the flute in the school band. Talk about gay. In registration Miss Campbell interrupts me telling Heather that I'd like to play but can't afford to and in Mrs McKay's next class I'm informed a spare instrument has been found, in a tone that suggests it's wasted on me. I take up flute mainly because I don't like to disappoint and I like showing off when I can. On the rare evenings Heather's parents take her out without me I practise at my own house which is so noisy nobody can hear me.

We each choose seven Standard Grades. I am in the top set for everything except maths where I'm on course for a shameful B. I am embarrassed to be in M2 and our teacher is Baldy Laing. He's the guy from the Hamlet cigar advert minus the jokes. He's introducing himself when the door flies open and dozens of ping-pong balls bounce in and I recognise my cousin Peter's laugh in the corridor. Each ball has a comb-over.

We all get a good look at his baldy head as Mr Laing bends down to pick one up. 'Silence!' He slaps the blackboard so hard with his pointer it rips.

We obey. He hates us all but he hates me most.

'You think you're clever, Mr Barr,' he says and who am I to disagree. 'You think you should be in the class above.'

At that I shake my head. I know I'm rubbish at maths.

This he takes as some kind of insult so I'm made to carry a desk out into the corridor and sit there doing sums on my own. Teachers walk past and do a double-take, not quite believing their eyes. Pupils on errands for teachers between classes smile at me, this might make be a bit cool. Miss Campbell, who teaches maths, is perplexed. From then on I'm always in the corridor of shame and one day Baldy Laing bawls at me for coming in to ask permission to go the toilet when I could just have gone without him noticing and I burst into tears and run down the corridor not sure where I'm going till I storm into Miss Campbell's guidance room and cry, 'I can't stand maths and I can't stand Mr Laing.'

He storms in after me and shouts, 'I can't stand that boy!'

Miss Campbell soothes us and somehow I end up in her maths class.

Me and Heather love science with its Bunsen burners and subatomic truths and take chemistry and physics. Biology is gross and also a bit too easy so we shun it. In a taster session about breathing we are given sheep's lungs to dissect. They're more grey than red and smell rotten but are still in working order as we see when Mr Garvie huffs and puffs into them. The whole class groans and gags as the gory bagpipe inflates and deflates. Mr Garvie wipes his lips and laughs. This is obviously his signature move. A knock at the door and he leaves class to take a message. When he's gone I nudge Heather and we look at gormless Leeanne Smith staring out the window. She's glaikit, totally not with it. She's even lower down the food chain than us because at least we're clever and can give the teachers lip, not that Heather ever would.

'Smith,' I say, surprised by the stiffness of the sheep's lung as I pick it up and hand it to her. 'Suck it.' She shakes her dumb head. 'That's what Mr Garvie's going to do when he gets back and if he sees you doing it first you'll get extra marks.'

Leeanne has never had extra marks. She was the last to read at Keir Hardie and probably should've been on the blue bus to the special school. She picks it up, rattling that feeble phlegmy cough she's always had, puts it in her mouth and sucks hard. Mr Garvie walks in just as she vomits. Unable to speak for sick she points at me but I calmly deny it and he won't believe her and nobody else volunteers blame so we all do lines for the rest of the class. No, biology's not for me.

Modern studies, moddies, is all about debate and I love it. Heather prefers places to politics so she takes geography.

Mr Roebuck, the moddies teacher, buys all his clothes from a charity shop to 'challenge capitalism'. We don't tease him too much about the fusty smell and big paisley ties because we like him. He's a rebel who lets us walk around class and go to the toilets without his asking permission. It was him who told me about *Spitting Image* and now I watch it every week on the portable in my room. He explains the issues behind the Craig's imminent closure and says that politics trumps economics. Mr Roebuck runs the debating team and the public-speaking team so I sign up for both.

One lesson he says we're going to have a special talk but we're not allowed to tell anybody else about it. Then there's a knock at the classroom door and in swagger two guys who remind me of Uncle Joe. They look us over and nod behind them to a shorter, slighter man with dark spiky hair and stubble. He seems familiar. They're all ancient, at least thirty. Pleased to have an audience he jumps on a desk and says that revolution is freedom and Scotland must free itself from Maggie and her unjust Poll Tax. We don't pay it in our house, not because we're rebels but because we're all on benefits. Same way we escaped the recession – you can't get negative equity on a Council house. Secretly I agree with a lot of what Maggie says – you should work hard, you shouldn't take benefits unless you need them, it's not wrong to want more. But the Poll Tax doesn't seem fair. The spiky-haired guy takes off his green Parka and he's banging his fist about taxing the poor to benefit the rich and we're all on our feet cheering when the door bursts open and Mr Margrave flies in all furious. For a second the two bigger guys don't know what to do but before we can blink Mr Margrave says quietly and firmly that he's 'very disappointed' and they're hanging their heads and

Mr Roebuck is wanted in his office. On the News that night I recognise our visitor as the leader of the Poll Tax Riots: Tommy Sheridan.

PE, home economics and tech are all remedial and drama is too gay even for me. Inspired by the Crystal messaging system which allows us to gossip with one another from any of the BBC Master microcomputers in the school, me and Heather take computing studies with Mrs Shaw who is new to Brannock. On her first day she wears knee-high boots and a pencil skirt. We test her as we do all new teachers. When she goes out we make paper aeroplanes and stick them into every inch of the ceiling tiles. She walks back in. We're all working at our computers keeping one eye on her. She says nothing. How can she not see the ceiling full of paper aeroplanes? One flies down on to her desk. She ignores it.

The bell rings and as we fumble for our bags and start to shuffle out she says, 'Forgotten something?' and makes each of us reclaim the plane we made from the ceiling, standing on chairs and desks to get it down. She knows she will make us all late for the next class and we'll all get in trouble. She is unbroken. Next time, when we're finished writing a number generator program in BASIC, she lets us play Tetris till the bell rings. Within a week of her joining Brannock she's spotted laughing in corridors with Miss Campbell. She won't take any crap but we decide we like her.

Our absolute favourite class is English (where we cry over Anne Frank so we choose French over German for our modern language).

'Give me a girl at an impressionable age and she will be mine for life,' sing-songs Mrs Kennedy on the first day of Standard Grade English. 'Or he.'

One wet Sunday I'm flicking channels and it becomes apparent that Mrs Kennedy has modelled herself on Miss Jean Brodie, the eccentric Edinburgh teacher in her perilous prime. The rrrrolling *Rs*, the immaculate coiffure, the overly personal anecdotes about her and her Harvey's trips to the theatre – we are her set! I rush to the phone, glad it's not cut off for once, and dial Heather's number so fast I get it wrong and when I do get through I'm so overexcited she thinks my mum and Dodger have finally killed each other till I explain and she rushes to her telly. We feel mildly cheated by Mrs Kennedy but decide not to let on. We are, after all, her *crème de la crème*.

'Defeat – I do not recognise the meaning of the word!'
Margaret Thatcher, quoted in *The Battle for the
Falklands* by Max Hastings and Simon Jenkins

WEDNESDAY IS THE WORST. Every Wednesday morning brings a benefits bonanza for my mum, Dodger and my uncle Joe – she gets disability benefits for the brain haemorrhage she had when I was nine. She calls this her 'Wednesday money' and queues at the post office to get her benefit book stamped by the woman behind the counter with the tight grey bun and tight grey face. I know she needs this money, I know she deserves it – she can't get on her bike and get a job because some days her balance is so bad she can barely walk. She's not sponging like Dodger and Joe. But I wish she'd spend it better, buy some shares in something or save up to buy our house off the Council. Make us rich!

All queues, even ones that promise to take you somewhere good, are depressing. This one is especially bad because everybody in it has something wrong with them or claims they have. Dodger's got a dot-to-dot scar round each shoulder where his arms join his body as if they've been stitched on. They kind of were after he fell drunk in front of a car. He wears a T-shirt that reveals his scars when he moves his arms, which he can now do easily and painlessly. My uncle Joe is a master of the art and, priest-like, dons a stiff white collar. He makes sure to wince slightly as he queues, leaning on the woodchip walls for support.

It's a wonder his back manages to hold him up as he walks down Newarthill high street past Streaks Ahead and into Bullah-Bullah's Paki shop for a carry-out: Buckie for the men and White Lightning super-strength cider for the ladies. My mum grabs a few token messages: tins and packets, nothing that needs actual cooking because she still hasn't learned. She struggles with a dusty brown paper sack of tatties and my uncle Joe, keen to start drinking, lifts them with just one hand. The act is over. I try not to look at Bullah's son Ahmed behind the counter because I know he'll tell everybody at school. Anyway, I think, how come he's got a full moustache at twelve?

I know the party will start when I'm still at school. I'll only be halfway through maths with Baldy Laing by the time Mum, Dodger and Uncle Joe are back at 15 Rannoch Avenue with their carry-out, the front door open to whoever wants a drink.

It's the dark green bottles of Buckie they love. Made by Benedictine monks in Devon, Buckie is a fortified strong red wine (15 per cent). Cranked up with caffeine, it's stomach-churningly sweet and stupidly cheap. When vomited up – as it always is – it hangs in glossy molasses-like strings, reeking like turpentine, that you've got to pull from your mouth. 90 per cent of the monks' brew is sold in a ten-mile area in Western Scotland called the Buckfast Triangle, where countless men disappear. Newarthill is right in the middle. It's unholy stuff and my mum's doctor prescribed it to her when she was pregnant with me to build her up. The monks we study in RE have consciences.

By the lunchtime bell they'll be on their third bottle. The music will be turned right up while me and Heather get our usual table in the corner and I eat my favourite lunch of baked potato, cheese and beans with a battered sausage.

By the time the bell rings at 3.30 p.m. Heather is giving me a look across French class that says soon it'll just be us. Everybody chucks their books in their bags and races out. They couldn't flee faster if the school was on fire, streaming out in all directions to Carfin, to New Stevenson, to Holytown, to homes where their parents wait with meals on the table. We're the last to leave and even Madame Auberge is itching to go. Heather and I are the only people going further into the school as we head to the library.

The library is two classrooms knocked into one and it's governed by the Dewey classification system and Miss Harris. The shelves are real wood and cover the walls from floor to ceiling so the books on the bottom get scuffed and the ones on the top get dusty. There are two BBC Master computers with monitors that flash green letters against a black background. The internet has yet to be imagined but for now a system called Prestel connects us to other schools. The gossip potential of this is huge but for now the books are more attractive than the computer.

Standing behind her counter, but barely taller than it, is Miss Harris. She knows me well as I've avoided PE here every week of every year so far on account of my 'asthma'. She's the only person I've ever met from Edinburgh. She has short, chalk-dust curls tight to her head and will always be a Miss. She still lives with her mother and every

Christmas buys a new Cliff Richard calendar for her office out the back.

Heather and I are still officially going out though neither of us is really clear about what this means. We hold hands a lot and snog (no tongues). We vie for top place in most classes. She's hasn't got a mousse-crunched spiral perm and her face isn't caked in pan-stick and she doesn't reek of Tribe or Exclamation! She's one of the cleverest, most beautiful girls I've ever met, the missing middle sister between Lucy and Susan Pevensie in *The Lion, the Witch and the Wardrobe*. Our relationship shields us both: me from being a poof (true) and her from being a virgin (also true). We know we love each other and we hate almost everybody else. Miss Harris is happy to grant us sanctuary and we talk to her about books. Only the cleaners are left when she packs away the date stamp and the ink pad that somehow never dries out. It's 4.30 p.m. and the coast will be clear of cretins so we can walk home safely. Even the Catholics from Taylor High School down the hill in New Stevenson will have walked up in their Rome scarlet uniforms. At the end of term the two schools send their biggest boys to fight and sometimes it turns into a riot. We walk downstairs and cross the echoing foyer without care, looking up at the gold-lettered board where we hope to see our names emblazoned as the first joint Dux. The double-doors swing shut and the janitor squeaks across the lino to lock them behind us. We walk up the steep car park where Miss Harris's white Nissan Micra waits alone. We watch her drive up Newarthill high street and beyond all the way to Edinburgh. Her brake lights blink a message I've yet to decode.

This Wednesday I decided I'm not going to Heather's house. The Ds are lovely but I eat into their kindness a little bit more every day even though they'd never say or do anything to make me feel awkward. Well, Mrs D wouldn't. I am, after all, her daughter's boyfriend. I feel the unique discomfort of a guest wearing out their welcome. I'm going to go home to my own house.

'Are you sure?' says Heather, her perma-pink cheeks blushing with concern.

'Nae worries, hen.' I butch it up, turning on my heel and swaggering off.

I hear it before I see it. Crystal Fucking Gayle is wailing and the front door is open, 'heating the street', as Granny Mac would say. Cigarette smoke chokes the air and I cough my way through and go straight up to my room where it's just as loud. I click my black-and-white portable into life and catch the start of 'Neighbours, everybody needs good neighbours . . .' There are two tellies in this house and this one is mine. Just like this bedroom with the locks I've fitted on the door is also mine, all mine. I can hear them and smell their smoke but they can't get in here unless I let them. Madge and Harold are having an argument about something to do with Charlene and my stomach is rumbling. It's Wednesday so there will be plenty of food, maybe even a Chinky with dark glossy noodles and chunks of what I hope is chicken.

Neighbours never lasts half an hour like it says in the paper so I creep downstairs just before six to sneak some food. No one hears the stairs creaking. I think about Pertwee my pet cockatiel passive smoking on her perch and decide I'll move her to my room. Through the living-room door I see: Uncle Joe dancing with Big Letty from next door, Dodger drunk in a chair conducting an imaginary orchestra and Andy teaching tricks to his Rottweiler Tara. No Mum. I am taking this in when somebody jumps out from behind the door.

'BOO!' he says and they all laugh. I dutifully jump. 'Come in the scullery wi me,' says this man I don't know. He rests his hand on my shoulder and says, 'Tall fur yer age, eh?' and turns me round, pushing me into the scullery and kicking the door shut with a flick of his foot. The doors are only cardboard so the noise is barely muffled.

'Ah jus want my tea,' I say, rhyming 'want' with 'pant' so I don't sound like the punchable Public Speaking Competition winner I am.

'Git me a can and we'll hae a wee talk,' he says, showing surprisingly white teeth.

I wonder if they're falsers like my dad's. Wanting to get away but feeling pleased he's trusted me with this manly request, I step towards the fridge-freezer.

Cold dawn is breaking behind the fridge door and spilling across the floor when he's on me, grabbing my arms and wrapping them round the fridge-freezer while pushing his thin hard body against mine, his crucifix belt buckle stabbing into the small of my back. I've barely had time to shout 'MUM!' when he pulls the freezer door open and shoves my head in.

To be fair, I wasn't expecting that. I start kicking my feet but to no avail because I've taken my shoes off in the house – I obey the rules even when nobody else does and Granny Mac says you shouldn't bring dirt indoors on your feet: 'Think where they've been.' If you'd only been on the street at the front of her house you'd be fine because she bleaches it every day straight after scrubbing her steps. So I am kicking behind myself with the holey smelly socks of a fourteen-year-old. I can only kick with one foot at a time because if I lift both feet off the ground there's nothing to support my neck and I half hang myself. My feet don't connect with his legs and he pushes even harder. He's shouting something but I can't really hear for the blood booming in my ears. Inside the freezer his words settle alongside a lone pea trapped in permafrost for ever like a lost polar explorer.

So here I am.

These are the last things I will ever see: the empty plastic ice-cube tray where I once experimented with cryogenic suspension of bumblebees, Hans Solo-style; the hieroglyphic stickers of a chicken, a leg of beef and a fish, each with the maximum number of months they can be stored in here, and a box of fish fingers, with the bearded Captain Birdseye girning for ever.

I'm not sure how much air is in here and I curse myself for not paying more attention in maths because if I had I'd be able to calculate the volume and work out how much time I'd got. By the way, I can now reveal the answer to that age-old question – the light does go off when the freezer door closes. I won't be able to share this fascinating discovery with anyone if the man jamming my head in the freezer has his way.

I stop shouting for help when I realise (a) I am using up air, (b) I am panicking myself into an asthma attack, (c) the insulation is coffin silent and (d) nobody partying in the living room can hear me over the sound of Crystal Gayle crying because some man made her brown eyes blue. The white-rubber seal around the freezer door sucks at my neck like some satanic school tie. My long-awaited Adam's apple pushes against it, creating a gap so I won't suffocate. I hope it doesn't pop back in.

I'm standing, up with my arms wrapped round the fridge-freezer like it's the world's clumsiest, fattest dance partner. My head is jammed in the freezer bit atop the fridge. The stranger is thrusting against me. This is something I've imagined in my bed at night or practised with Mark. This guy has to be in his thirties. He's got curly dark hair like a Spanish conquistador and that rarest of things in Scotland – a tan.

'Sunset yellow E110'. My eyes find words to comfort me. My glasses flew off when the door slammed on the back of my head but the box of fish fingers is close enough to read. I think of sunshine and fish and the two colours just don't match. Also, why would something that lives under the sea need or want to be the colour of sunshine?

I scan the list of ingredients in an instant but that's all the reading matter in here so I start finding words within the words. 'Shin', 'shun' and 'sine' come out of sunshine with minimal effort. The pressure on my neck is now continuous and I think I feel my lips turn blue. This moment lasts for ever. How long will it take, I wonder? There's no chance of a responsible adult coming to my rescue – there won't be a responsible adult in this house until the money stops and the hangovers start. He chooses only the best for the Captain's table, does Captain Birdseye. Him and all those boys on a boat. Just like Captain Hook. Breadcrumbs, maltodextrin, sunset yellow E110, the bees that didn't come back to life when I defrosted them.

I don't know if it's been seconds or minutes or hours or months – maybe there should be a little picture of me on the inside of the door with an indicator of how long I'll keep in here before going off. Then, as suddenly as he appeared and grabbed me, he's gone.

I can't feel the belt-buckle in my back. I daren't move in case it's a trick. If somebody walked in the scullery right now they'd think I was just standing with my head in the freezer casually hugging the fridge and question the widely held belief that I'm a clever boy destined for better things. I let my stiff, sore arms flop by my sides. He'd act now if this was a trap. But nothing. What if he comes back even harder? I clocked his biceps. He can push as hard as he wants. My arms dangle by my sides and I allow myself to breathe deeply. Air opens my windpipe, pushing against the seal, easing the freezer door open ever so slightly. I count down loudly from ten thinking I'll turn around and surprise him at THREE. I can't stay here in the dark for ever with Captain Birdseye. But what if he's looking for a sharp knife to finish me off? Good luck to him, there's nothing sharp in this house and probably for that reason. I was fucked when it came to making the Advent crowns on Blue Peter. Not that my parents ever bothered giving permission. For once I was glad. 10, 9, 8, 7 . . . sunset yellow, sunset yellow, 6, 5, 4 and THREE! I lift my hands up and swing the door out thinking I'll hit him if he's standing there, buying me enough time to get out the back door and down the road to my dad's. A seven-minute run with fourteen-year-old legs. The door hits the side of the fridge so hard it bounces back clouting my head.

More Scooby-Doo stars. I reach in and snatch my specs and slap them on my face. The metal frames are even colder than my face. I spin round. He's gone. Unless he's hiding under the sink with the Vim I'm the only person here. Then, slowly, the scullery door opens. I press myself back, storing up potential energy to spring for the back door, when my mum walks in. She's pink from outside.

'I've been up the road tae git yous weans a Chinky,' she says, still at the happy stage. I know she'll want a cuddle and I'll smell her sweet boozy breath. 'Not wantin' a Chinky? Ye makin' yer own tea, son?' she asks, walking towards me, her eyes the colour of the pilot light on our rarely used gas fire. 'Good boy, but ah'll do it, you do yer homework.'

I am pinned against the fridge-freezer by something like love. I tower a foot above my mother.

She reaches up past me to the freezer door, opens it and takes out a packet. 'Fish fingers?'

12

'Economics are the method: the object is to change the soul.'

Margaret Thatcher, interview for the *Sunday Times*,
1 May 1981

I 'M ON EVERY TEAM at Brannock High School that doesn't have anything to do with throwing, catching or kicking a ball. It's not that I'm competitive, it's just that I have to win. Everything. As far as I'm concerned, an A is just an A+ waiting to happen. Maths doesn't count (and neither can I). And I'm not just on the teams, I lead them: it's a captain's life for me.

'It's all about being the best consumer,' explains the homely home economics teacher, Miss Kane. Renowned for failing to keep discipline in her totally doss subject, Miss Kane is nevertheless one of the school's sweetest and kindest teachers. She looks like a baker's wife and her floury cleavage invites you to sob in it. Because it doesn't take too many brains to scramble an egg or stitch a tea-cosy, home economics attracts plenty of remedials. I will not say I am proud of the day Heather and I replaced Leeanne Smith's baking powder with washing powder but I will say it was funny watching her watch her sponge cake bubble out the oven. Because we're clever and very well-behaved we escape without suspicion, letting somebody stupid take the blame.

Home economics and tech (what my dad called wood-work) are only compulsory for the first two years of high school. These are not star departments. So Miss Kane is giddy with the chance of fame offered by the Young Consumer of the Year Quiz sponsored by the utterly privatised British Telecom.

'Doesn't being the best consumer just mean consuming the most?' I ask Miss Kane, who sees me as her last best hope.

'No, Damian, it's all about "knowing your rights and responsibilities as a consumer",' she reads from a leaflet emblazoned with the BT Tower in London, which I've seen on the News. It seems the only big building not yet targeted by the IRA. We don't get bombed up here, we're too close to Ireland. '"It's a fun, challenging and interactive national quiz which tests pupils on a wide range of issues including consumer law, food and health, safety and the environment, managing money and finance, credit and the European dimension. It will make them more aware of their consumer responsibilities and rights."'

So far my responsibilities as a consumer are limited to making sure my mum, Uncle Joe and Dodger put back all the 50ps they've taken out the gas meter before the inspector makes his monthly call. That and making sure my mum buys enough phone stamps on a Wednesday so our phone doesn't get cut off and I can keep making my endless, obviously essential calls to Heather. Maybe I can win phone stamps this way?

'But isn't consumption a disease, miss, like in *Wuthering Heights*?'

'Don't be clever, Damian,' she snaps, before realising she needs to keep me sweet. You catch more wasps with wine than vinegar, says Granny Mac. She smiles and delivers her killer line: 'We need a captain.'

I'm in.

At fourteen I am finally embracing the fact that I'm always going to be a geek so I might as well be the absolute number one geek. The geek, I write on the back of my timetable, will inherit the earth.

'And the national final will be held in Brighton.'

Brighton.

She might as well have said the Emerald City. Brighton exploded into my mind when I saw the bombed hotel on the News in black-and-white all those years ago. The day my mum left my dad for Logan. It's the place where Maggie proved she was indestructible and somehow it's held responsible. Brighton is a bad boy. If Brighton was a pupil at Brannock High it would hang out at smokers' corner.

According to the papers, Brighton has the highest incidence of AIDS in the country, which means a high concentration of homos.

'I'm in,' I say, as if there was ever any doubt, and set about forming my team. Heather is obviously Deputy Captain and between us we feverishly discuss who will make the cut and how best to play them off. We've got three places to fill and need knowledge spanning all the areas Miss Kane highlighted. I'd love to ask Mark so we could run away to Brighton together but he's still treating me like I don't exist. Scott McAlmont is one of the best runners in school but also a computer geek, which cancels out his athletics points. We reckon he can be corralled, PLUS Heather has a slight crush on him. Choosing him would make me feel less guilty about her wasting her time with me when she could be losing her virginity. That leaves two spaces. Me, Heather and Scott all like John Jackson who's really good on politics even though he always stands as a Tory in class election and only ever gets one vote: his own. And he votes to save Maggie Thatcher in the balloon debate. Not surprisingly, he lives in the new Brosley Estate where the Bing was. Secretly I admire him for standing up for what he believes in, even agree with some of it but couldn't admit it. Plus I like his flat-top which reminds me of the guys from Big Fun. He's in. We all agree our fifth and final space should go to a girl in the interests of feminism, which we've been learning about in moddies. The only girl smart enough but sufficiently unpopular to have the time to memorise the Sale of Goods Act is Sonia Morrison. She is just massive tits. Straight As and double Ds.

We have our team.

Miss Kane approves, not that I would change it for her anyway, and looks pleased with her chance to finally show the rest of the school that home economics is good for something other than leaded scones and knitted atrocities. I've got another trophy to win and the chance to escape to Brighton. If I can just get there I'll find other people like me and Mark. This thought is thrilling and terrifying.

We practise every Wednesday after school with a man from the local Trading Standards called P-P-Peter. We finish all his sentences for him to save his stutter, which sharpens our buzzer response times.

'Who is the G-G-Governor of the B-B-Bank of England?'

We don't have actual buzzers as the school budget's been cut again so we shout 'BUZZ!' Miss Kane bakes us a perfect Victoria sponge.

'BUZZ! Eddie George!' shouts Scott, always the fastest.

'Translate from the L-L-L –'

'Latin,' I interrupt. 'BUZZ! *Caveat emptor*! It means "let the buyer beware".'

For their prep I assign each member a different newspaper each week. This is hard because we can't get our hands on broadsheets in Newarthill. Bullah-Bullah only stocks the *Daily Record* and the *Motherwell Times* so we rely on Miss Kane to visit the John Menzies in Motherwell and bring us back the *Guardian*, *The Times* and the *Financial Times*. Like yuppies we pore over the business pages, learning about privatisation and inflation and deciding whether or not the UK should join the EMU. Maggie is against it. Kinnock is for it. I'm unsure. Friday nights we gather at Scott's house in Holytown because his parents have got a satellite dish so we watch the Business News on Sky and then *The Simpsons*. After that we drink Tango and play *Golden Axe* on his Amiga – to sharpen our reaction rates, obviously. Between games we speculate on what we'll be asked and who we'll be up against. Heather sits next to Scott on his bunk bed and I see that's how things should be. Sonia makes eyes at me and I make faces at John.

When quiz day finally dawns we're so over-prepared we could probably win a case in the small claims court after beating the Stock Exchange. We know our rights and we're prepared to fight for them! To present a united team we all wear our navy-blue blazers with the gold badge saying *Concordia*. My frayed cuffs crawl up past my wrists. I pull them down hoping nobody notices. We sit in the school minibus in silence and disembark at Motherwell Civic Centre. The quiz is in the echoing Council Chamber where I annually puff myself up for the Public Speaking Competition. Last year I spoke about the nightmare of yet another family Christmas with the same predictable gifts, the same boring relatives and the same endless meal round the same old table – all made up. I half convinced myself. Anyway, I won.

Our opponents are Dalziell High School, which, they constantly remind us, is correctly pronounced 'dee-ell'. The nearest actual private school is in Glasgow but Dalziell pupils have a whiff of the grammar with their shiny hair and pink cheeks that say rugby and too posh to get preggers. Their captain has actually turned up the collar of his school polo shirt. Of course they're not wearing blazers, they don't need props. I hate him and I want to be him all at the same time.

Our audience is a very nervous-looking Miss Kane and P-P-Peter and that's it. I'm excited to spot a reporter from the *Motherwell Times* and swear I won't wear an anorak when I am a journalist. Both teams pretend not to mind the lack of spectators. Our hands hover over actual buzzers.

Question 1, Round 1: 'What is the current interest rate?' BUZZ! Dalziell are straight in with '15 per cent'. Sonia wobbles nervously and Scott looks ready to sprint. The next question is about food colouring and I BUZZ! in with 'sunset yellow E110'. Fish fingers. Rounds flash by and soon it's a tiebreaker. I hold my sweaty palms a single cell's breadth from the buzzer.

'Finchley is the parliamentary constituency of . . .' I BUZZ! and lean into the microphone.

'Maggie, Maggie Thatcher.'

'That is correct and I believe that makes Brannock High the winners!'

'Y-Y-Yes!' P-P-Peter's pride echoes round the empty chamber as Mark tries to get his arms round Sonia who wobbles uncontrollably and we all do high fives and Heather throws dirty looks at a stunned Dalziell.

P-P-Peter's boss at Trading Standards presents prizes and looks pleased with the future of capitalism. We pose for a picture in the *Motherwell Times* in branded Young Consumer Quiz T-shirts. We're given the 'very latest in communication technology' – my heart leaps at the thought of a mobile phone but no, it's a phone card. A close second. Dalziell pretend to look pleased with runner-up mugs. Elated, Miss Kane takes us all to the newly opened McDonald's where we toast our win with root beer and pretend to get drunk.

When I get home that night nobody cares what I've done or won that day. The music is so loud they don't hear me come in and my mum's passed out so I show Dodger my certificate and he grabs it off me and dances about with it and I try to grab it back and it rips and he just throws it on the floor and laughs, stamps on it. Tears fill my eyes and he shouts 'Boo-hoo' after me as I run upstairs. I've had enough. That night when everybody's passed out and the music's finally stopped I decide to make the phone call. I've memorised the number off the telly – 0800 1111. I don't want anyone to overhear this so I sneak out to the phone box at the top of Rannoch Avenue. It's one of the old-fashioned red ones and I wish it was a Tardis. Shaking, I dial the number. Somewhere far away it rings and I expect Esther Rantzen to answer.

'Hello, ChildLine.' It's a friendly English voice, a woman. Not Esther.

I say nothing.

'Hello? What's your name?'

I tell them my name is Luke in case they can trace me. I

starting telling her everything from Logan on and she says slow down and I tell her how bad it is for us weans in this house.

'Why does your mum call you Wayne, Luke?' the kind lady asks.

'No, she doesn't call me Wayne, I am a wean,' and I try to explain that 'wean' is the Scottish word for child but still she doesn't understand me. I tell her about Dodger and how much I hate him for causing all the fights and getting my mum into drink and she says slow down and then I hang up feeling guilty for telling her anything. I should've kept my mouth shut. What if they recorded me? I wander the streets for an hour or two then go home to bed.

It's a full month until the Strathclyde Regional Final and we up our revision at Scott's to three nights a week. Mr and Mrs D need a break. Scott says his parents always wanted more kids so we assume they're pleased by five loud hungry teenagers. I bet they wish we were out drinking cider and sniffing glue. I'm just pleased to be out the house.

Strathclyde is the biggest unitary authority in Europe, it's probably bigger than Belgium. It includes Glasgow and over 1 million people and every single constituency in it votes Labour with Motherwell North having the highest majority of all. If John Jackson was eligible to vote he'd double the Tory's local tally. Because of this, Maggie hates Scotland, that's why she tried the Poll Tax out on us. It seems she'll never go. We watch the news for our revision and it's always strikers chanting 'Maggie, Maggie, Maggie, Out, Out, Out!' Except for John we all join in. But it doesn't feel quite right – hating her just helps me fit in. I don't need to stand out any more: six foot tall, scarecrow skinny and speccy with join-the-dots spots, bottle-opener buck teeth and a thing for waistcoats. Plus I get free school dinners and I'm gay.

We trounce our next opponents so soundly I forget who they are. When I'm sure they can't catch up I actually answer a question wrong just to make them feel better. Heather, Scott, John and Sonia turn as one, knowing full well I know salmonella is the bacterium in eggs made famous by Edwina Currie. Miss Kane actually cuddles P-P-Peter as our prize is announced: an all-expenses-paid trip to the national finals in Brighton.

We've got to get parental permission to go. As usual I fake my mum's signature – all crippled capital letters, one leaning into the other but never joining up. These days I try not to correct her when she gets simple sums wrong or forgets names or dates but sometimes I can't help it. The unfairness of her condition and her refusal to make it better by stopping drinking make me so angry I press through the paper. I could ask her permission – she'd never stop me doing anything academic because 'school'll take ye far' but why should I? She doesn't ask me if she can have another Diamond White. So I fake her signature and take my spending money from the gas meter like everybody else.

At the train station I can't believe I'm finally leaving Motherwell, leaving Scotland. I've never been further than Glasgow. Our destination is London King's Cross where we'll change trains for Brighton. It seems unbelievably far away but I can't get there fast enough. Miss Kane, P-P-Peter and Mrs D are our responsible adults. It might as well be the Orient Express. As we go through Carlisle I realise I've left

Scotland and I squint at the countryside flashing by, hoping it's different. Until now Mrs D is the only English person I've heard who wasn't reading the News. I wince at how harsh we sound compared to all the English around us. I sit facing forward, willing the train to go faster. King's Cross is a blur of platforms and people, more people than I've ever seen. I point out a black man then worry he saw me pointing. We catch another train and soon we're leaving London, moving into bright green countryside and I'm surprised cos I thought it was all cities down south and then we run out of land and we're slowing down.

Seagulls greet our train. Even they sound English. I jump off the train and run ahead desperate for it all first – to steal the joy and make it my own. I flash my ticket at the barrier without stopping, like I travel all the time, and note the vaulted ceiling which contains more sky than there is in all of Scotland. Bursting through the entrance I actually jump and try to click my heels like they do in films. I want somebody to see me arrive but nobody looks twice. I almost run into a man talking casually into a brick-like mobile phone like it's something he does every day. He has to be at least thirty. He smiles at me and turns away without breaking his important-sounding sentence. I move closer and breathe in, deeply, desperately, trying to catch a whiff, convinced it will be Calvin Klein. All I smell is the sea.

'We're not in Kansas any more,' I say without really knowing why and sigh dramatically as if I'd walked all the way here.

'Thank God,' says Heather, suddenly by my shoulder.

She smiles and hands me my bulging schoolbag then takes my hand and we walk ahead of the others to the taxi rank.

Any illusions of staying in a suite at the rebuilt Grand Hotel are banished when we head out of town to the Halls of Residence for Sussex University. This is my first visit to an actual uni. Me and my mum watched *Brideshead* together so I expect Sussex to look like Oxford. There are no spires, no pretty boys on bikes. This is more like Motherwell Civic Centre with its purpose-built concrete bunkers. The library, we're told, looks like an open book from above. The seagulls must be well-read. We've got our own rooms and a shared scullery. I'm desperate to see Sebastian clutching Aloysius but there's not even a *Young Ones* punk – they've all gone home for the Easter holidays with their washing.

'C'mon, time for dinner,' announces Miss Kane.

We pile into two taxis and head for Brighton where we're promised whatever we want. This will take my restaurant meals to ten and I can still taste each one course by course. It's been a long day and it's getting dark but we're determined. Up ahead Brighton Pier flashes out of the night, plunging straight out to sea. It's a long finger dripping with diamond rings beckoning us in. A brightly lit merry-go-round spins twin-tub fast. I realise I've seen it before – there's a poster of it in Miss Campbell's guidance room. Our taxi driver doesn't notice any of this and stops at a red light. Not one of his passengers has eyes for the road. As the light turns amber I spot a nightclub called Revenge. The queue to get in is all young guys and some of them are holding hands. They're not scared-looking or even acting ashamed. I worry for them. Amber goes to green and I stare at them through the rear window as we jerk forwards. I feel myself blushing and blinking.

We take the biggest table at the Chicago Rib Shack and I confidently order sticky ribs followed by Mississippi Mud

Pie. We're each allowed a shandy. I panic when the bill comes in case I have to pay in 50ps and what if I've not got enough but Miss Kane pays.

The quarter final is the next day at the Brighton Centre. It's big and grey and ugly like the uni and sits right on the seafront like some huge experimental seashell. This is where Maggie gave her 'I will survive' speech the day after the IRA bombing. I'll be sitting where she stood.

We queue with all the English schools and everybody sounds like *Grange Hill* or *The Famous Five*. Heather is checking out the competition. I'm busy scanning for obvious homos but what would I do if I found one? All I can think about is Revenge.

Our match is up first and we're against the other Scottish teams: The Borders, East Lothian, West Lothian and the Highlands. 'Tcheuchters,' Mrs D mutters, happy not to be in the minority for once.

The winning team – us – will go on to the semis and ultimate glory. A rumour sweeps the hall that a celebrity will present the prizes. This breaks down the barriers between schools and we rush from one team to the next: 'Her from *Blue Peter*', 'The guy from *Knight Rider*', 'Roland Rat', 'The Governor of the Bank of England', 'Madonna!' and finally 'Maggie Thatcher'. All seem possible.

The buzzers connect to a flashing scoreboard. The quiz master is a local DJ doing his best Bruno Brookes impression. Maybe it is Bruno Brookes. Everybody and their responsible adults crowd into the cavernous hall to gauge the questions and the competition. Miss Kane, Mrs D and P-P-Peter beam from VIP front-row seats. I think I see the man from the train station three rows behind and I smile. A stranger stares back.

'An appropriate question,' says the DJ, shuffling his cards and grinning plastically. 'In what year was the Act of –' BUZZ! and East Lothian lights up.

'The Act of Union was 1707,' sing-songs their captain, her Edinburgh accent as foreign as any English.

The first round is all about Scotland and we're clearly not patriotic enough. I curse our curriculum for including only English history. My knowledge of Scottish monarchs is limited to a rhyme Teenie taught me: 'Mary, Queen of Scots got her head chopped OFF' and on the 'OFF' you decapitate a dandelion with a flick of your thumb.

At the end of Round 1 we've yet to score. 'Plenty of time,' says the DJ. Heather flinches. Maybe our buzzer isn't working? Four rounds flash by and the only one we get is 'negative equity'.

'And in last place it's Brannock High School,' says the DJ, with a final shuffle of his cards.

'We are the champions!' sings bisexual Freddie Mercury over the loud-speakers. I try not to look bitter. I never lose and what I'm really losing is Brighton – the final is tomorrow and now we've got no reason to stay. We've only got accommodation so long as we're in the competition. Heather nudges me into sporting applause. We won't be meeting any celebrities. I will never get Revenge. As we trudge off we're handed an envelope, probably our train tickets. I open it and out falls a Virgin voucher for £50, more than I've ever had. I feel a bit Wonka. Straight away I know what I want.

After a sombre lunch of fish and chips on the pebbly beach we go to the Virgin Megastore. We snigger at the name. Heather is studying the cassette singles when I point to the videos. My mum doesn't like me watching Channel 4 after that time she turned on *My Beautiful Laundrette* and we both had to sit there because if one of us turned it over it meant acknowledging something. I sneak bits late at night with the volume right down, and watch all of *The Lost Language of the Cranes* in near silence. Virgin has a section with a big GAY sign but I can't go there. I rush straight past to the books. Heather knows what I'm after and finds them first. I hover, afraid to place a hand on the glaring cover. 'Go on,' she nods. I pick it up and nothing happens. I grab the next one and the one after that until I've got them all. We'd tried to get them out of the library but it didn't stock them, wouldn't. Heather pushes me towards the cashier, a girl, thank God. I blush as I hand her the vouchers. Do I want a carrier bag? Yes, thank you. I linger but all she says is 'Next' so we rush off giggling and join the others heading for the train station.

'What did you get?' asks Miss Kane, eyeing my bag.

'Oh, it's a present for me,' lies Heather and I take her hand and we smile at each other and can't wait to read *Tales of the City*.

13

'You may have to fight a battle more than once to win it.'
Margaret Thatcher, *The Downing Street Years*

T HE SECOND TIME I try to kill a man I'm fourteen. Killing a man seems a very grown-up thing to do – like writing in biro. That night I stand outside myself watching myself doing the thing I always knew I was going to have to do. There are no surprises. Not yet. It's OK, I think, I can square it with the police and other authorities. There's no greater authority in the land than the Prime Minister and I can make Maggie understand. She knows the value of education and I'm a Grade A student who has never been in trouble before. I'm a Young Consumer.

It's after midnight on a Wednesday night and as usual everybody's out cold: sleeping where they fell. All the lights are blazing and the cassette is straining on its spool as I pick my way among them, a scavenger on a battlefield. Some change has fallen from Uncle Joe's pocket but I know he counts every penny so it's not worth stealing. Big Letty has gone back next door, keeping up appearances. Nobody moves. Only my mum has made it up to bed. Yes, Wednesday is definitely the best night for this job.

I've dialled 999 more times than I can count for the police to come and break up fights between men and women who five minutes ago were best pals, more maybe. Sometimes they send a fire engine as well and our neighbours stand on their front step tutting as the blue lights dance across their faces. The police know us now and greet me by name.

Handcuffs are to Dodger what my dad's watch is to him. Even so, my mum says she loves him. 'Dodger's not a bad man,' she says. But he does bad things. He doesn't work, he's never sober and he never knows when to shut up so he's always fighting someone, usually my mum. They spin together, a mess of limbs, kicking and biting and scratching and swearing and it's all OK the next day, only it's not. 'His daddy was a drinker,' says my mum, like she never touches the stuff. 'And his mammy too.' One night Dodger and his brother and his daddy and his mammy went beyond their usual beyond. 'She went to poke the fire and fell in,' says my mum, raising her hands. 'Puff, her nightie went up! That was that.'

This, I think, would stop me drinking. Not Dodger. He's not stopped since. His own worst enemy. Mine too. If I can just get rid of him, I think, the parties will end and my mum will stop drinking and things will get better. Our house will be quiet, normal, safe.

I tell myself I'm doing the right thing as I slip out of bed. Outside the fug of my covers it's cold because, as usual, there's no money for the gas meter. The other single bed lies empty, accusing me of selfishness, but I don't care – I need my space. One by one I pull back the three nails clawed over my door before slipping back the bolt I bought myself from B&Q. This is the oldest door in the house – the only one to survive since it was built, solidly, for coal miners. When we had miners. The other doors are flimsy and most have been kicked or punched in, their cardboard honeycomb hearts on show. Not my door, not my room.

Standing on the landing, I crack the door to my mum's room. In the only double bed in the house she lies alone – her tiny body barely interrupting the blankets, her small silhouette just visible in the dirty orange light shining through her curtains from the streetlamp outside. My mum, struck by White Lightning, totally unconscious but thankfully not naked. Her eyes, that high unhealthy watery blue of one who nearly died, screwed shut beneath thin almost see-through lids. Her tiny fists, nails chewed to nothing but still painted bright red, balled up like a baby's. A martyr to 'her nerves'. She's no danger, I think as I close the door, to anybody but herself.

Across the landing in the last of the three bedrooms Teenie has rolled into a corner facing the wall, her unbrushed blonde hair covering her face. She's nearly as tall as me now, captains the netball team. 'You read enough for the two of us,' she says when she gets her report card, the lone A for PE. She wants to join the Army when she grows up. I've lost track of who's got custody of Billy but he's at Logan's tonight. Next to Teenie snores Tricia who's only ten but wearing a bra in her sleep. In the other single bed sleeps her older brother, Shawn, and their younger brother Aidan. They're always being suspended and will soon be expelled. The air is sweet with dried piss from rubber sheets. If they wake I'll hear their sheets squeak. I will make quiet work.

I pad downstairs. There's no need for me to creep quite so theatrically but that's what they do on telly and that's how I imagine Lady Macbeth did her deed. So I creep, brushing my hands along the spiky Artex walls. I remember the one and only time my dad came to the house and caught Dodger laying into my mum and pulled him off then picked him up and smashed his face into the Artex wall, grating it like cheese. He's collected us from the bottom of the street ever since, when he turns up.

There are fifteen stairs. Each one seems to move below my bare feet but that's only the carpet slipping because my mum laid it herself. With my other hand I grip the banister to be sure I don't fall and wake anyone.

My room key is balled in one hand the way I sometimes hold my balls. Comforting. Slowly I ease the living-room door open.

Most of one whole wall is window but the Venetian blinds are drawn. Our house is the only one on the street to sport this seventies fashion and it embarrasses me that people walking by can tell we're poor just by looking. Even old Mrs Buchan across the road has fancy ruched Austrian blinds. Not us. The dirty heavy Venetians, once white but now smoked the yellow of dirty teeth, are staying put – this way the party can go on all day and night without the neighbours seeing in. Of course, they can hear everything. My mum is unashamed – doesn't give a fuck what they think, she says. There's only one person she cares about. Granny Mac often does the rounds of her brood scattered in the surrounding streets. Walking past 15 Rannoch Avenue she can hear evil but there's no need for her to speak of it so long as she doesn't see it. The Venetians are like the curtains at confession. I am glad of them tonight.

Here and there, the surprisingly sharp metal shafts are bent where somebody's fallen into them and tried to grab on. 'Fucking red hand of INLA,' Dodger calls it. The same dirty orange light seeps its way in from outside (a sodium light, I learned in chemistry).

Joe's chunky bulk eats the length of the couch, rising and falling as he snores. I know he's naked beneath the blanket because his Y-fronts are on the floor. For a second I think about peeking but resist because if he wakes and sees me standing over him the whole house will be up and I'll get a kicking and then everybody will know for sure what they think they know already.

As if he's been dropped from above, Dodger sprawls in the armchair in the corner facing the telly. The national anthem has long since finished and the Union Jack has flickered away. I'd not seen an actual Union Jack until I went to Brighton. Red, white and blue. The telly whines like a dog waiting to be let out. I click it off. Dodger is wearing snow-wash denim jeans frayed round the ankles and a white T-shirt stained by the strings of black drool slabbering out his mouth. Not a thin delicate trickle but thick sticky strands like the stuff that comes out the fat Baron in *Dune*. He's spewed on himself as he does most Wednesdays. His tongue is tarred black but it's not with Mrs Rayson's Black Jacks. It's after midnight and he's not asleep – he's unconscious. The top of his head, bald now, shines in a shaft of light from the blinds. He's still not actually ugly with his big brown eyes but maybe his very unScottish tan is actually just his liver giving in. But he's ugly when he's drunk and that's most of the time. I lean right into his face – closer than I've been to any man before. Closely packed stubble pushes through his skin. His black breath bubbles up at me in a burp and I gag silently.

I pull myself together – if I get hysterical I might give myself an asthma attack. I turn away from Dodger's slipstream of Buckie sick and take a deep breath. Time for action. I've got to be calm. *If it were done when 'tis done, then 'twere well it were done quickly* . . . I memorised this for English.

I feel cold even though, some miracle, the radiators are ticking into life, the pipes protesting at unfamiliar heat. I need all this to be over. The weekly cycle of feast or famine, from empty cupboards to full stomachs as they drunkenly order another Chinky banquet to celebrate what? Another Wednesday? Another party with the same songs ending with the hiss and burble of walkie-talkies as the police arrive, embarrassed, to disentangle another 'domestic' while me and Teenie stand in the background, hands over our ears, too bored to cry, wondering where's Billy, where's Billy?

In Barlinnie or wherever I end up I'll get three square meals a day. As a murderer, I will command respect – other prisoners will go quiet when I walk into the dining hall. I will be able to read in peace in my own cell – the door locked reassuringly from the outside. I will have clothes that keep pace with my growth spurts and nobody will laugh at me for being unfashionable because we're all dressed the same. Teenie will probably go and live with Granny Mac and my mum, when she's calmed down and sobered up, will see I've done the right thing. I did it for them too.

I don't want there to be blood – I've seen enough to know that lots of blood doesn't mean definite death. If I use a knife he might grab it from me and the blood on the floor will be mine and that's not what I want.

Strangling seems sensible. A table lamp lies on its side behind the couch Uncle Joe is snoring on. The 40-watt bulb is singeing a brown silhouette through the pink nylon shade. I flick the switch off and knock the lamp. The bulb pops and broken glass tinkles. My heart pounds a Black Box beat so loud it's got to wake them. I'm panicking in the half-dark, lying on the floor behind the couch, terrified to look up in case I see Dodger looking back at me. He's quiet on his feet, always sneaking about. 'Sleekit,' says Granny Mac. I peek over the top. Nothing. Nothing stares back at me. Working quickly I pull the plug from the wall and loop the plastic cord round my arm like Granpa Mac winding the cable from his lawnmower. When it will go no further I pull once, hard enough to detach it. The cheap *Made in China* crap holds for just a second and I lay it quietly on the carpet. Now I've got my motive and my weapon.

The same shaft of light picks out Dodger's bald patch. I can't see his face at all now but that suits me. He didn't stir when I broke the light bulb so he's properly out. A car passes outside, its headlights briefly illuminating the living room. I think about running out and stopping them and telling them everything and driving away to a new life where parents wag their fingers and children roll their eyes and families go on holiday together. I see it all in the last few seconds before I become a murderer: the post-party chaos, every surface covered with empty bottles and overflowing ashtrays that will soon be sifted for butts. A crime scene already.

I pick my way through the mess, imagining how clean it will all be when I'm done. I won't be in jail for long. I've planned the letter I'm going to write to Maggie. She's going to get me out. I am acting as an individual – I am taking responsibility for improving my lot. With the letter I will enclose photocopies of all my report cards and hope she overlooks the remarks about me being a chatterbox. I will also include clippings from the *Motherwell Times* about my achievements as Captain of the Young Consumer Quiz team. I am a more-or-less model pupil – I do library duty, I don't fight, I don't drink or smoke or sniff glue and I am NEVER going to get a girl pregnant. Granny Mac says it's wrong to wash your dirty linen in public – that's what confession is for. But I'll have to tell them why I did it. My public speaking and debating skills will be handy then. I'll be sure to make eye contact with the jurors and speak slowly as I explain how I was driven to it, how it was the only thing I could do to make it all stop – to give me and Teenie a chance of a normal life. Maybe we'll get custody of Billy. I want to contribute to the state instead of being dependent on it. I want a mortgage and shares and nice things with statutory guarantees. This is the only way for us to be a family. Maggie will understand and if she needs any persuading I think Esther Rantzen will support me. Maybe they can call ChildLine and get transcripts of the call I made to them?

Now I'm standing over him. I can't hear my heart any more. I'm not even sure I'm breathing. After this I will be a saviour. A hero. I'm doing the right thing, I tell myself, as I wrap one end of the cord round each hand to make a loose noose. Dodger's head slumps forward. I plan to call the police as soon as I know he's really dead and tell them everything so they can take my willingness to cooperate into account. I've got nothing to lie about. They've been here before, they know the story. They'll be sympathetic, probably grateful. Joe snores on.

Not wanting to give Dodger any chance to wake I pull the noose totally tight straight away. The plastic digs into his stubbly neck, his head snaps up and his eyes pop open. No, they're already open. They've always been open. I keep pulling, tighter and tighter. The plastic warms and slackens in my hand. Fuck! Fuck! It's stretching. Elasticity is a basic property of plastics – I know this from physics. It could snap. He could live! I pull harder and it must be working cos he puts his hands up and pushes his fingers between his neck and the cord. Air gets inside him. He's staring at me and his eyes are bulging. The streetlight shines in his eyes making them yellow. A stupid grin splits his face. Quietly, he starts laughing.

Then he hisses, 'Wit you gonnae dae, eh? You gonnae cull me? Eh? Wit you gonnae dae, eh?'

I pull harder and harder but his fingers are there now and the plastic is slackening and my hands are slippery with sweat. I nearly stop then he says, 'Wit you gonnae dae, eh, jessy?'

At that his face blurs into Logan's as I pull and pull and pull and he sniggers under his stinking breath like Muttley the Dog and he shouldn't be laughing by now, shouldn't be breathing.

He lets go of the cord and drops his hands and dares me: 'C'mon, nancy boy, do it!'

Now there's nothing stopping me. I really could kill him. But I don't. I can't. Not because I don't want to – but because he does.

I drop the cord and it drapes round Dodger's neck. He's not laughing now. My hands throb as the blood comes back and I wish for my old mittens.

'Back tae yer bed,' he whispers, jabbing at the ceiling and rubbing his neck as if he's just taken his tie off after a hard day at the office. 'Night night, sleep tight.'

Joe snores on.

I walk back upstairs, not bothering to be quiet, and push my hands hard against the sharp Artex, feeling the pinpricks of plaster pierce my skin. I close my bedroom door, turn the key, slide the bolt and replace the nails. I look at the blood on my hands then turn out the light.

14

'Children who need to be taught to respect traditional
moral values are being taught that they have an
inalienable right to be gay.'

Margaret Thatcher, Speech to Conservative Party
Conference, 9 October 1987

F OR MY SIXTEENTH BIRTHDAY I am given wings. I've
begged for an aviary ever since Charlie the Canary and
my dad has finally given in and built me one. I hand him his
tools and it's the longest we've spent together in years. I love
being close to him even though he doesn't say much. He
doesn't say much to anybody, it's nothing personal, I know
that. After two days of huffing and puffing and hammering
and nailing it stands stinking of creosote in our back garden.
My stomach turns at the all-too-familiar acridity: it remembers being pumped all those years before.

'Yer a cuckoo right enough,' says my dad, handing me the
key for the shiny new padlock.

The aviary will be perfect when the smell goes. Uncle Joe
'found' some railway sleepers for the foundation, he's handy
like that. I went with my dad to the B&Q by Forgy to get the
rest. He smiled down at the cashier and she blushed up at him
and the whole lot was 50 per cent off and I worried we'd get
stopped as he filled the car boot. The black-felt roof slopes

backwards and you can open the plastic windows to keep it dry and well ventilated. Cages run along one side from waist to ceiling and the shiny steel bars ping off the front for easy cleaning. I've got enough room for about thirty budgies. Nearly too many to name but I'll still give them all names and talk to them and listen when they talk back. I'll keep them safe. Most importantly I've got my own space outside the house with a lockable door where me and Heather can just hang out. We won't need to burden her mum and dad quite so much.

Now I just need some birds. Pet shops are pricey, you're better off going to a private breeder, says Danny's dad, who still keeps canaries. He tells me to get the *Scot-Ads*.

This mustard-yellow classifieds paper comes out every Wednesday. It costs a pound and my mum always buys it before blowing the rest of her money. 'Early bird and all that,' she says, tapping her nose, sure of a bargain. It's like the Holy Ghost Fathers' Garden Fête only she doesn't need to move from her chair. She doesn't read out loud any more but she still moves her lips as she intones like she's praying. In these yellow pages she's found a second-hand Kenwood mixer (still in box), a nest of three glass-topped chrome coffee tables (only one chipped) and Lucy, our West Highland terrier (possibly too feisty). I turn my nose up at second-hand. I want better things than *Scot-Ads*. I want new things.

When she's finally finished haggling in her head I'm allowed to take it out to the aviary. My mind flutters with what I might find as I flick to the 'PETS' section. The bottom right-hand corner of each page, where my mum has licked her finger to turn it, is blotted and sags off. That's how cheap *Scot-Ads* is. Under 'BIRDS' there are blue, green and opal budgies. All pretty enough, but I want a lavender and they're rare. I'll have to keep looking. Disappointed, I start lining the bird cages with the paper, scanning the other sections as I go. There are dodgy-sounding motors, designer jeans that no longer fit and Council tenants hoping to swap houses. The last double-page spread is headed 'CONTACTS'.

Here it seems people are on offer.

'31yo guy seeks VGL female 25–35 for fun. No kids.' What kind of fun? '55yo lady seeks solvent gentleman to treat her right. Smokers welcome.' 'BIG Girl About Town, size 18, 5'10" seeks man who can handle her.' There are columns and columns and each one has a box number you can write to if you're interested. Dozens of someones each seeking a some-body. There's a handy guide to decoding: 'VGSOH' is 'very good sense of humour', 'NS' is 'non-smoking', 'ALA' is 'all letters answered'. There's no explanation of 'VWE'. A box at the bottom warns that you must be '18yo' to place an ad or reply.

Near the bottom of the list the ads turn 'GAY'. I feel a shiver of recognition and shame for something I've not yet done but already know I will. 'Married couple after bi fun. Daytime only.' 'Young gay guy seeks active older.' Active how? 'Bored of scene 25yo seeking LTR with genuine guy.' What scene?

There are five 'GAY' ads and they're definitely not going on the bottom of a birdcage. I think about showing them to Mark but he's still sneaking off in his lunch hour to have sex with that fat forty-year-old when her husband is out at work. He's told everybody, the whole school knows she starts crying when he climbs off her to put his uniform back on. I don't believe he's turned straight, not really. I haven't, as much as I want to. I still smile at him and he still ignores me, walks past. I still miss him.

That night I pull the nails over my bedroom door and sit down to reply to all the ads except this one: 'Gay pensioner seeks grandson for discipline.' The terms and conditions warn you must be twenty-one or over to place or reply to 'GAY' ads because that's the legal age of consent. Get caught doing anything underage and you're both off to jail. I click to select the black ink from my multicoloured pen and in my neatest handwriting begin 'Dear Sir'. No, too formal. Ripping the top sheet off the lined A4 pad, I start again. 'Dear Mister'. No. Finally I settle on 'Hello, my name is Damian. I saw your advert in the *Scot-Ads* and I wanted to get in touch . . .'

Before I know it I've covered one whole side. It excites me to think that a total stranger will suddenly know about me. It's the same impulse that makes me sneak downstairs at night and quietly ring random long-distance numbers, muffling the dial as it spins, just to hear the foreign voice on the other end, another voice in another world. Sometimes I say 'Help me' and hang up. Mostly I say nothing. My eyes are automatically drawn to the digits of my dad's number which Mary the Canary refused to give me but which I stole from her by looking over her shoulder at the dial when she rang him for a lift home when she took me shopping once. She was tipsy that day and didn't catch me spying.

The men I'm writing to aren't a million miles away. They're right here in Scotland. They might even be in my village. They might read between the lines and work out where I live and track me down and kill me but hopefully not before we've had sex.

According to my letter I've left school and have a job in Motherwell. I sign off 'Yours sincerely' and read through the whole thing again. Clicking the pen for red ink I draw a box on the bottom right-hand side and write down my height, hair colour, eye colour and build: six foot, dirty blond, blue, slim. I can't afford the £2 to get photies done in the booth at John Menzies in Motherwell so I'm hoping the description and my age (twenty-one) will be enough to tempt a response. They can't all be dirty old men and if they are my age will definitely work. I copy the letter out four times, practising my signature differently each time, and address each envelope to the right advert, making sure I've not accidentally replied to a full-figured older lady seeking afternoon SM. *Scot-Ads* assures all readers they will send any responses directly in a discreet brown envelope. I don't get much post but I've started to send off for university prospectuses already so I can pretend it's one of those when it comes. If it comes.

I wait. And wait. Monday, Tuesday, Wednesday, Thursday and Friday. The lips of our letterbox remain sealed. At lunchtime on Friday Heather demands to know why I'm so moody. I haven't told her about the letters but she knows something's up so I just say 'Home'. That's explanation enough. Who wouldn't be stressed out by 15 Rannoch Avenue compared to the wall-to-wall carpeted sanctuary of the bungalow her dad built with its well-stocked cupboards, Shield-blue bathroom suite and utility room with dishwasher? She looks at me sympathetically and I feel familiarly guilty.

I want to tell Heather the truth about me. I want to tell her everything, I do. I hate lying to her. But I'm scared she'll think I don't love her. I do love her, really love her, just not like that. And I don't want her to think I'm using her, wasting the time she could be with other boys. So I drop hints here and there, test the water. Heather buys me a ticket for New Kids on the Block – it's our first concert – and we both scream just as loud for Donnie Wahlberg. I'm taller than most teens and my waving hands hit the spotlight and for a second my shadow covers the arena, briefly brushing Wahlberg's face.

I keep my vigil by the letterbox and finally a reassuringly anonymous brown A4 envelope addressed to me plops through. I can tell from the heft I've got replies. I can't take it to school because if someone steals it I'm dead so I slip it under the door of my aviary for later. Moddies is a jiggling leg, chemistry is doodling atoms, double maths is an eternity of equations, and even English can't end fast enough. That day I skip the library and tell Heather our homework 'n' gossip session is off because I've got a migraine, which is almost true. I've got to get home to the letters, to read them and reread them and find the man who'll take me away. For the first time ever I join the newly freed 3.30 p.m. crowd rushing home from school and I look just as excited as them.

Back at 15 Rannoch Avenue I go straight round the back to my aviary and lock the door behind me. Carefully I unstick the big brown envelope. Inside are four smaller envelopes, all different. All four have replied. Four chances! I feel like Cilla Black on *Blind Date*. I choose the smallest first, carefully slitting it with the Stanley knife my dad left. I scan the whole thing quickly, not daring to let my eyes settle on any one sentence in case it disappears. It's in tiny script and covers one side of the sort of writing paper Granny Mac uses to enter tiebreaker competitions in *People's Friend*. It's from a fifty-four-year-old man called Fergus who admits he said he was thirty-five in his advert because he didn't want to put guys off. He likes under-twenty-fives and he's into school role-play with him as the pupil.

Fergus is a no.

The second is in a thicker envelope that suggests a birthday card. It's sealed with a kiss. The handwriting is loopy and the dots over the *is* are bubbles, possibly even deformed love-hearts. David! Left school at sixteen and is a trainee hairdresser. David LOVES Kylie, Jason and Sonia! Anything Stock Aitken Waterman! He LOVES the scene but recently fell out with his 'sister' so he needs a new one. How do I do my hair? Am I passive or active? Who do I fancy off *Neighbours*? Who knows about me?

David is a reluctant maybe.

The third envelope is so thin I could probably read through it if I held it up to the light. Inside, the paper is ruled with thick black lines, like bars on windows. Paul is writing from Barlinnie – the Glasgow prison that my uncle Joe avoids. Paul did say he was after a penfriend in his ad but seriously . . . He's using up his paper allowance on me so he really hopes I'll write back. He doesn't say what he's in for but he does include a picture. More like a mug shot really, him staring straight into a camera, an evil Mr Potato Head.

Paul is a never.

The final envelope. Will there be a golden ticket? Soon I'll have to go in for tea, my mum will be surprised I'm not at Heather's. The house should be reasonably quiet as they're all reasonably sober cos they've no money. Unless they've raided the gas meter again. It's a Tuesday so it'll be tinned soup or something. I don't care. This is worth it.

In envelope number four I find Johnny Kendall.

Johnny is a yes.

We exchange two letters within the first week, always to the PO Box, although he asks for my address. I agree to meet Johnny at midnight the next Wednesday. He'll be driving a white H-reg Rover 'like the ones in *The Bill*'. I tell him to park by the gates of Keir Hardie Memorial Primary School, thinking it's just far enough from the house. Johnny says he's thirty-one, five foot ten, rugby build, dark brown hair, butch. He's too 'discrete' for a photie.

Crystal Gayle is wailing on and on and I want to smash her face in and it won't be long before Mrs Buchan next door complains again. She goes to chapel with Granny Mac and word will get back and there'll be another scene. Dodger never gets tired of Crystal Gayle or Daniel O'Donnell or Rosemary Clooney and he's the only one who can work the stereo drunk. We might get fewer complaints if he picked better music. Unnoticed, I walk straight out the front door to a rousing chorus of 'Danny Boy'.

The streets are sleeping as I slip along the road I used to walk to school. A couple of houses are as lairy as mine and I keep my head down. I look over my shoulder to make sure I'm not being followed and as usual I'm slightly gutted to find I'm not. By the school gates I see red brake lights glowing in a white car, warning me away and luring me in. This is it. I can still turn back and never reply to any of his letters and that'll be that.

Johnny jumps when I tap the window. Good, he's nervous too. He leans across and opens my door. He's fat. He said he had a rugby build. I just stand there. The car smells of something that isn't Lynx.

'Ye getting in then?' he asks. 'It's cold.'

I get in and he starts the car.

'Stop!' I unclick my seatbelt. 'Where are we going?'

He's going to abduct me, kill me, I'll be a face on *Crimewatch UK* like that Jason Swift boy – don't have nightmares. I should never have come, this is what I deserve.

'Just a wee drive.'

'Where?'

'Where d'ye want tae go?'

Nobody has ever asked me this. 'Strathclyde Park,' I say, using my lowest voice and trying not to hesitate. There's the reservoir, the remains of a Roman Baths and a tacky wee fairground that's the most exciting thing for miles. It's a place for kids and I feel like I've given myself away.

Johnny drives and asks questions and I give him yeses and nos.

'Ah thought ye'd be mair chatty from yer letters,' he says, as we wait at a traffic light by the Craig. I'm paranoid my dad will see me and sink low in the seat.

'Naebody's gonnae git ye,' says Johnny and I look at him. 'Not even me,' and he laughs and puts a CD on.

The lights are still flashing when we get to Strathclyde Park but the big wheel is still. We sit and watch it and talk and eventually I manage whole sentences. After about an hour Johnny asks me what I'm doing at school.

'English, maths and –'

He laughs. 'So you don't work in Motherwell then.'

'I do.' I feel myself blush. 'I do!'

Indeed I do. This bit is true. I work part-time as a waiter at the New Lotus, got the job through a girl called Deirdre I met sewing gingham scrunchies at Young Enterprise, an after-school club for fourth-year pupils from schools across the area. YE is all about being entrepreneurial. There are ten of us in our company, eleven if you count the poster of Maggie still hanging on the wall of the office where we meet. Heather is the Production Director, Deirdre is the Marketing Director and I am the Managing Director of our accessories company. We sell shares in our company for 5p. After disagreements over labour conditions and a failure to launch anything that anyone wants to buy, we fold but I stay pals with Deirdre, who gets me a job with her at the New Lotus. She shows me how to write chicken chow mein (no onions) in Chinese script and warns me to decant the unused cream from the individual cream portions into a big jug lest stingy Mr Weng docks our wages. I love talking to the customers, feeding them. I got fired from being a paper boy cos I read the papers instead of delivering them. The New Lotus is my best job yet.

'I get sausages and chips in Chinese gravy for my lunch if I work day shift.'

'Is that right?' says Johnny. 'Ye like sausages, eh?'

He stares at my crotch. The doors are locked.

I ignore his question and babble on about the New Lotus. I like when families come in for birthdays. I turn my jealousy into extra good service and they tip me and Deirdre shows me how to hide tips in my socks. I tell him about the fish tank in the store room upstairs. It's six foot long and the glass is green with algae and the water is so murky you can't see in and there's only one fish left and it's the size of the tank. In another corner there's a sort of altar that Mrs Weng keeps with a fat Buddha and a golden cat with a waving paw and tangerines spiked with smoking incense sticks. I tell him how the chefs are always losing money over dice. Once I nudged their table and changed the result and got chased and a massive shiny cleaver thrown at me. Johnny rolls his eyes. To keep him listening I tell him about the time I was stood there waiting for an order when I felt a draught and looked down and there was my knob sticking up over my belt – one of those hard-ons I get all the time for no reason. He's interested again. I finish that story fast. 'Nobody saw.'

'So what school d'you go to then?'

I say nothing.

'Ye don't look like a Catholic so I'm saying Brannock High.'

I say nothing and tell him about my girlfriend Heather and he hangs his head over the steering wheel laughing. I talk and talk and he listens and listens and I barely stop for breath. He just listens and smiles and I like it when I make him laugh. He doesn't try to kiss me which pleases and disappoints me. What's wrong with me?

Every Wednesday night for the next month Johnny picks me up in the same place and we drive off to Strathclyde Park and talk. He doesn't ask why I don't let him pick me up at home because who would want their sixteen-year-old son getting picked up at midnight by an older man in a fast car? I tell him I've got to get back and he believes me even though I know nobody will miss me. I love that he thinks my life is normal. I wish he was better-looking. If I'm going to be caught being gay I'd like it to be with a man who's handsome. I'm sure he wears mascara. Will I have to wear it too?

Johnny is full of tales. He says that a famous footballer goes straight from Ibrox to Bennett's every Saturday night.

'What's Bennett's?'

His pinkly shaved double-chin Jabbas with excitement. He smells of Joop! which he pronounces 'jewp'. Chunky thighs flex in tight white jeans: fat people always have strong legs. He's got a squint so he can keep one eye on me and another on the road. Lights flash through the sunroof, reflecting on his scalp through his already thinning hair.

'What's Bennett's? What's Bennett's? Bennett's is the scene, Princess.'

The scene.

He agrees to take me the following Friday.

'Have ye never heard of ABBA?' Johnny asks as we set off for Bennett's, his voice veering into disbelief, feeding the steering wheel smoothly through fat fingers as he turns right on to the motorway.

'Who?' I ask, noting with relief the signs pointing to Glasgow. So he's not taking me somewhere remote where in a few months I'll be found in Lego-limb bits by a nice retired couple walking their retriever.

'ABBA! Ye better get used to them.' He turns them on and the song is 'Dancing Queen', young and sweet and only seventeen. Da dum, da dum, da dum. He thinks I'm twenty-one. I think he's thirty-one.

I push myself back into the white leather seat as we hit 60 then 70. Nobody noticed me sneak out but my mum will miss me if I'm not there for school in the morning. She still gets us up for breakfast.

'Don't look so worried,' he says, fisting us up to fifth gear. 'My dad's in the polis, we'll not get done if we're stopped.' No murderer would admit that, would they? He glances over. 'Oh they're gonnae love you at Bennett's.'

ABBA are facing their Waterloo cos Johnny stops the CD player and I'm impressed that he's got one in his car. His driving is flawless as you'd expect for a driving instructor taught at seventeen by a policeman dad. Moving faster than you'd think for a fatty, he nips round to my side and opens the door, waving me out on to an imaginary red carpet. I could stay in the car, not get out, and tell him to take me home. He puts his hand out and I take it.

'Welcome, Princess.'

The bouncer is brutal. His head is shaved so close the bristles could brush you to death. The slash-in-a-tomato mouth has never smiled and the sentry eyes stare dead-ahead. He stands with soldier-polished black Doc Martens planted shoulder-width apart that would be happier in your face.

'Jinty!' sing-songs Johnny, extending his hand to be kissed like the Queen.

What kind of a name is Jinty?

Instead of breaking it, the bouncer plants a courtly kiss on Johnny's Claddagh ring.

'Johnny, darlin'! Long time no see!'

All eyes are on me and a curious queue builds up behind us.

'Ah've brought a wee chicken.' Johnny points at me. I smile, trying to be casual but confident, and keep my buck teeth behind my lips.

'Pouty!' says Jinty and elbows me, knocking me into Johnny. 'And what's your date of birth, son?'

Before I can calculate an answer Johnny's straight in with '20th June 1974. He's eighteen.'

Jinty leans in for a closer look and laughs. The queue joins in.

Johnny turns on the guy behind him. 'Shut it, queen!'

'If you say so,' says Jinty.

Johnny mwah-mwahs him on both cheeks without even bothering to check no one's looking. Jinty pockets a folded note and waves us in.

'Have fun, ladies!'

We're buzzed in the door and check our coats.

'Her bark's worse than her bite.'

'Whose?'

'Big Jinty's.'

My face says everything. 'Her? Is she not a man?'

Shivering, but not because it's cold, I follow Johnny up a dark staircase. The carpets are sticky and bass music is pounding. The tune gets clearer as we get close to the top. 'It's the rhythm of the night, yeah yeah . . .' Johnny pulls me blinking up the last couple of stairs and pushes me in front of him through a pair of double doors.

This is the rhythm of the night.

I'd love to tell Mark about Bennett's but he still ignores me whenever I try to talk to him. I'm bursting to tell him we're not alone, there are others like us, a whole secret world in Glasgow, but whenever I try to talk to him he swishes past, leaving me swaying and smarting in his Lynx-scented wake. He actually minces but nobody notices. Maybe all this would make him stop. Johnny uses a whole new language. I'm a PRINCESS or a CHICKEN. Everything is DEAR or DARLIN'. His highest compliment is CAMP. He is SHE and normal people are HETTY BETTY. He doesn't say GAY or HOMO he just say SHE'S ON.

Johnny turns up at school one lunchtime.

'What is it?' asks Heather. We're in the physics lab on the top floor and I'm sure I'm going to get a B at best.

'Nothing,' I say, turning away from the window where I've spotted the big white car parked in the bus bay out front. It looks whiter and bigger than ever. I'm sure the whole school has seen it, knows my secret.

'Liar,' says Heather and goes to look. 'What is it?'

'See that car?'

'Uh huh.'

Mr Viner interrupts our conversation. As good students we're allowed to get away with a lot but staring out the window and gossiping when we should be at our desks tackling elastic collisions is taking the piss.

'I'll tell you later.'

The bell for lunchtime goes and I can't decide what to say to Heather. What will work this time? What lies have I already told? What does she know? So I decide not to lie – I decide to tell her everything. It's like confession without the Hail Marys. As usual, she listens quietly while I go on and on. I make it clear I've not done anything with Johnny so I can always say I'm just experimenting if she reacts badly. We're hiding in the computer studies room to be sure nobody else hears us. When I finally finish she says nothing. Her cheeks are pinker than usual. That's it. I've lost her, my best friend, my only real friend. I'm alone.

Then Heather smiles and I think I always knew she would and I love her even more than I ever did and she says, 'I knew it.'

15

'I was sick at heart. I could have resisted the opposition of opponents and potential rivals and even respected them for it; but what grieved me was the desertion of those I had always considered friends and allies and the weasel words whereby they had transmuted their betrayal into frank advice and concern for my fate.'

Margaret Thatcher, *The Downing Street Years*

I T CAN ONLY BE spunk. I steal glances at the glistening pearly glob on my sleeve, not wanting to draw attention. We're taking turns reading out lines from *Macbeth*. It's Act IV. We're seventeen years old and about to sit our Higher exams but we still snigger when one boy has to read out a bit of Lady Macbeth's part.

I can't just lift my sleeve to my face for a closer inspection. That would get me looks. Holding *Macbeth* open on my desk with both hands I lower my face to the close-printed page as if I'm studying the footnotes, trying to get into the meaning. Once down there I catch the familiar ferny bleach and bananas tang. It must be a stray spray from my morning wank. Careless.

'Damian Barr, sit up!' clips Mrs Kennedy in her snippiest 'I expect better' tone. I pretend to yawn and pass my sleeve by my face. Yes, it's definitely spunk.

'Bored, Damian?' Mrs Kennedy enquires, her finger holding her place on the page, pointed but not painted nails stabbing a soliloquy.

Even though I'm part of her special set Mrs Kennedy must, as she's explained, be seen to treat us all equally. She can't have obvious favourites. In our evenings me and Heather sit mock exams and do our now-perfect Mrs Kennedy impressions but in class we must be pupils, not pets. When English is our last period we wait till everybody's gone and walk with Mrs Kennedy to the tiny English department staff room. Smaller than us both, she trots to keep up. There we marvel at the individual coffee cups, each teacher has their own and through them we try to divine the secrets of the drinker. Only Mrs Kennedy uses a teacup and saucer but she is Head of Department. Dainty pink roses clamber round the rim but not too wildly. Paper folders suspended on hooks line the walls, a story for each pupil, their ending predicted in As and Bs and Cs. Shelves sag with copies of the standard texts. There is a *Great Expectations* with the improbable Pip and next to him is the unlucky Tess who never stops walking. I pick up a paperback of *A Streetcar Named Desire* and consider how Mary the Canary was basically Blanche: thick with make-up and lies. She's gone now. My dad packed her bags a couple of months ago when she stayed out for a week after one of her gigs. The suitcases looked like a magician's luggage, all sparkles and silk scarves and secrets. Maybe after all this he'll finally take my mum back but no, he's had enough of women, he says. I can still smell Mary in his house: Poison by Christian Dior.

I consider slipping *Streetcar* into my bag even though I've nicked one copy already. I put it back and feel virtuous instead. After I breeze through my Higher I will walk in here with my books to my chest, Degrassi Junior High-style, and take my place, maybe with my own mug. Even if it's just me and Heather, Mrs Kennedy has committed to run the advanced CSYS class. Then we will say what we feel without being laughed at by a classroom of cretins. We will drink instant Nescafé then rinse our mugs and hang them on their own hooks over the sink. We will bring Tunnock's Tea Cakes and insight.

For now, I've got to get this spunk off my sleeve before anybody spots it. If I wipe it on my trousers I know it'll leave a shiny egg-whitey smear. It'll be round the school in no time. The chances of getting caught are increasing every second. My only hope of avoiding a mega-slagging and historic shame is to get to the sink in the corner of class and rinse it off – it's nearer than the toilets. I raise my hand.

'Yes, what is it, Mr Barr?'

'Miss, I –' and I slap my right hand over my mouth, push myself up with my left and start retching. For good measure I puff my cheeks out.

Seats are pushed back from desks and the class inhales as one. Mrs Kennedy jumps up to her full four foot ten inches as I bolt across her classroom with both hands over my mouth, stick my head in the sink and booooooooak!

Breathing deeply between fake retches I pick up the faintly fireplace smell of the cracked cube of pink carbolic soap that will never ever run out. I turn the tap on and splash water over my sleeve, heaving dramatically so that no one will want to come and look over my shoulder. I stand up and slowly wipe my mouth on my sleeve then poke round the plug hole for non-existent chunks. Such a considerate boy. I'm so convincing I actually start to gag. Mrs Kennedy hovers a safe distance away.

'Go and see the nurse,' she says, flapping towards the door, not wanting to touch me. Maybe this fear of mess is why she and her beloved Harvey have never had children. I don't need to be told twice. Out. Damned. Spot.

Down in sick bay Mrs Gordon, our school nurse and the member of staff with the biggest tache, is nowhere to be seen. I squeak across the lino and swoosh open the pea-green curtain round the bed hoping to catch her napping and then what? She's not there. The Dettol air smells delicious. I bounce on the edge of the bed, which sits up as a proper hospital bed should. I kick my shoes off and slip in like sliding a Twix finger back in the packet, careful not to ruffle. My toes find the hospital corners. I could lie here for hours, days. I could live in this silent, antiseptic sanctuary. How long before anyone finds me? I'm sad to miss the rest of Mrs Kennedy's class but nothing was worth the shame of getting caught with spunk on my sleeve. Heather knows I wasn't really feeling sick but now I know I can tell her anything she'll be appalled and amused in equal measure. We'll roll around her bedroom floor screaming and her dad will burst in and tell us to be quiet and when he bangs the door shut we'll weep hysterically into pillows. My secret is now our secret. And we've got another ally: Mark is back. Two has become three.

I lie in sick bay staring at the pock-marked ceiling tiles wondering if they're asbestos and consider another wank. The fact that Mrs Gordon's mother goes to chapel with Granny Mac is enough to put me off. Tight between the sheets, I let my mind wander to my favourite books.

Catcher in the Rye with its pale yellow cover, the handwritten title scrawled and confidently underlined by a teenage hand still excited to have traded up to pen from pencil. I've folded every other page for future reference, underlined every other line with a note, usually with an exclamation: 'Sarcastic!', 'Satirical!' and, best of all, the newly discovered 'IRONIC!'. With piercing insight on page seven I observe that 'use of the first person makes things more emotive'. Soon after I'm clutching my pearls at Holden's 'vulgar language!'. Holden is 'contemptuous!' of Mr Spencer who fails him in history: 'It is all right with me if you flunk me though as I am flunking everything except English anyway.' Imagine having the courage, or luxury, of failure. If I don't get good grades I'm stuck here. For ever. 'I am quite illiterate but I read a lot' elicits from me an 'OXYMORONIC!'. Delighted to be able to use another of the terms Mrs Kennedy has taught us. I pay no attention to the second-last line: 'Don't ever tell anybody anything.' Like Holden I rise above all that 'flitty' gay kind of behaviour, or try to, because shouldn't books be better than people? On the title page I write 'Moral decay'. Holden's? Mine?

Since Johnny turned up at school in his big white car I am 'out' to Heather. 'Out' is a new expression and we love using it. I feel relief when I see her now. Whenever someone calls me 'Gay Bar', Heather and I trade looks. It would blow their tiny minds if they knew I went to an actual gay club and danced with actual gays. I want to tell them all about the scene, make them feel shut out of a world they don't know exists. At this point standing up in the foyer and admitting that I am what I am would really be a technicality. Letting Mary the Canary dress me up as Alexis Colby for the school sponsored walk in my second year was some-thing of a give-away. I arrived at school in full rouge, fake eyelashes and curled hair. At lunchtime I changed out of my uniform into a lacy black two-piece suit with pencil skirt and shoulder-pads then tottered three miles round the res-ervoir at Strathclyde Park, my toes crushing into the front, slipping and sliding in Mary's tights, her gusset munching at me. Heather held my hand all the way. I still feel a phoney. 'I feel sorry for Holden. He is just SUCH a damaged indi-vidual,' I write at the end of chapter ten, my biro exhausted by empathy.

The Color Purple is another set text I've practically memor-ised. It brought Mark back to me. Me and Heather were sitting in the English staff room waiting for Mrs Kennedy when I decided to look in my file hanging on the wall. It was unexpectedly heavy. Inside was a book. I opened it and immediately recognised Mark's bubbly girly handwriting: 'To my best friend and my greatest inspiration. *Make-da-da*. "You and me us never part". I love you, Damian Barr.' The promise Nettie makes to Miss Celie before their stepfather banishes her! He loves me! I showed Heather and she just shrugged, remembering the milkshake on her legs.

'See! He wrote this! I told you!'

That lunchtime I walk over to Mark, with the book in my hand, and he doesn't walk away, doesn't laugh at me, just smiles. Hair still perfect Jason Donovan curtains but skin barely scarred by acne. Compared to my lankiness he's short and tight — flick-flacks across the foyer and swims every weekend but he's stopped running, stopped competing. He's gone from an A to a C at best, from the athletic track to smokers' corner. His studliness is legendary after he got caught doing that housewife when her husband came home early from work. He wore his black eye like a medal. He is unassailably cool. Though Miss Harris did say she'd seen him in the library lately but never when I'm on duty with my date stamp and ink pad. I've been following what he reads on his record card. It's smarter than the stuff he gets a couple of classes below me where he shouldn't be.

'I'm sorry,' he says, by way of hello.

'You should be.'

'I am. Honest, I am.'

He's ignored me every day for over five years but I forgive him just like that. Because he wasn't really ignoring me, he was ignoring himself. I'd tried and failed to do it too though maybe not as hard as him. From then, when we're on the scene or with Heather, we call each other 'Sister' like Nettie and Miss Celie. Heather has forgotten, or at least forgiven, the milkshake. She isn't jealous and I love her even more for that.

Friday night is our night and the only night we all feel free. When I finish my shift at the New Lotus I change into something tight that I've bought from Burton's with my wages and get the train to Glasgow where I meet Mark and Heather. I down a bottle of Kiwi and Melon 20/20 on the train to catch up with them and we all bounce into Bennett's, paying twice on the door for our youth. Mark goes to the bar because he's the prettiest and gets served the fastest and we ignore the dirty looks from Johnny in the corner. We're done with him now. We only drink from bottles because you can't be sure about the glasses. We scrutinise every face on the dance floor. We watch for lesions. Has he got it? Has she? Do women even get it? We speculate wildly about who is doing what to whom and imagine what everybody at school would say if they could see us now. All the men fancy Mark but I don't mind because he makes them buy drinks for all three of us. Then Madonna comes on and we're Vogue-ing our arms off because this is the one place where we can get away. It's called a dance floor and here's what it's for, so, come on Vogue! Sister!

The one book I've stopped reading is the Bible. The spines of the primary-coloured Gospels from the Scripture Union are now as creased as they will ever be. For years and years I've prayed and prayed to Jesus to make me like everybody else so they would like me or at least stop hating me. At Keir Hardie I kneeled down in assembly and at Scripture Union, bowing my head and steepling my fingers, asked Jesus to get my mum and dad back together, to heal my mum, to strike Logan down and make me normal. I used to be like everybody else. At Brannock there are no prayers in assembly, we don't even pray in number one doss subject RE with the acne-scarred Miss Mackie who actually cried when we Frisbeed a yarmulke when she was explaining about Judaism. She got her own back, sliding an acetate of Auschwitz on the overhead projector.

I still say my prayers every night in bed, usually out loud cos I can't hear myself think for Teenie and the cousins bouncing on the beds next door and Joe and Letty and Dodger and my mum shouting over the music downstairs. I am careful to wank before I pray so I've no sinful thoughts in my head. I know off by heart the bits of the Bible that condemn me. Thanks to Leviticus and Revelation I know all about hell, the real hell that burns hotter than the smouldering fires beneath the Bing or the white-hot furnaces of the

Craig. As a homo I will be outside God's love – unwelcome at Scripture Union, barred from church and chapel, turned away from the gates of heaven by a celestial Big Jinty. I'm starting to think maybe Jesus wants me the way I am. After all, he can do anything he wants – he walked on water, he raised the dead! His dad made the world in seven days as a side-show to the ever-expanding universe. I want to do stuff with boys. Surely that's not my fault. Isn't everything God-given? Everything including AIDS – the punishment for not resisting temptation. I feel doomed in this life and the next.

Lying in sick bay I decide there and then that I have to break up with Jesus. After years of praying and being good I'm getting nowhere. I've got faith but I'm rapidly running out of hope. As for charity, I did that sponsored walk and me and Heather do the Oxfam 24-Hour Famine every year – surely the biscuits we sneak can't count against us that much? I didn't win the Dux at Keir Hardie but I've got As ever since and me and Heather are on track to be the first ever joint Dux, our names engraved in gold on a board in the school foyer for ever. I've been good. But still, I'm gay.

I close my eyes and say the Lord's Prayer as usual and then I start another prayer. I tell Jesus that I love him, I really do. I love him for dying for our sins, for bleeding on the cross in Jane's gift shop at the Grotto. I tell him I know I am a sinner but I've tried, Lord knows I've tried, to be the same as everybody else. After Mark shunned me I started going out with Heather and didn't touch another boy for four years, not until Johnny told me it was time I did something for him and then, well, it was only about three minutes before I came in his eye and he fell off his bed cursing me. I even tried doing it with a girl to be sure.

It seems most of the boys in my year have had a go on Jacqueline Slattery – Slattery the Slag. She's a rite of passage: a provisional driving licence, your first drink, learning curves in Lycra. She's a year above us and bra sizes beyond all the other girls. Freckles struggle out from under her foundation and her long hair is pube curly. She smells of Body Shop White Musk and something like Granny Mac's scullery on a Friday. She wants to be a beautician. She's got a lot to learn.

She's a slag, a hoor and everybody knows it. But she's not bothered. Her mum doesn't let her out on weekends but that still leaves lunchtimes. It's as easy as being nice to her in the queue for lunch. Telling her I don't believe the stories, she's not a slag really and I know what it's like to be talked about, to be misunderstood. Try before you buy, I think. Maybe I can go through with this. Even though it's January and sort of snowing I suggest we go for a walk in the woods behind the school where everybody except me does cross-country. I hold her hand and we talk and she says she likes me and suggests we lie down. Walter Raleigh-style I lay my blazer on the long frosty grass under a bald hawthorn. She lies down and pulls her navy pleated skirt up over her hips in a horribly familiar way and, not wasting the movement, hooks her pants down. There it is, the fanny, the hairy pie, the legendary minge that all the boys have licked. I feel close to them and at that my cock twinges.

'C'mon,' she says. 'Ah'm fuckin' freezin'.'

Approaching it like a biology dissection, I delicately press the fleshy mound, noting the straightness of her pubes, and ever so slightly part the flaps. It's smooth and red like the inside of a balloon. Jacqueline looks bored and grabs for my crotch but falls back with a sigh when I start spreading her flaps. Then it happens. Like the New York streets in *The Equalizer*, steam wafts gently from the hot place between her legs. We look at one another through it. Before I can say or do a thing her pants are up and she's on her feet shouting at me, telling me not to tell anyone anything or she'll say I couldn't get it up. That's that. I feel even cheaper than her.

So, Jesus, I did Jacqueline Slattery to try and change because you weren't making much effort. Give me a sign, strike me down or miraculously transform me there and then from She-Ra into He-Man. I string the prayer out, keeping it going longer and longer, hoping he'll intervene at the very last minute. 'I really am going now . . .' But nothing. No response. No distant voice at the end of the line. So that's that. I'm sorry it's come to this, I say. It's not you, it's me. You won't change me and I can't change myself. What will happen after I die I don't know but I do know I've got to find a way to live here and now. I know you can't love me, it's not fair of me to ask. So this is my last prayer. It's over for you and me, Jesus, just like it was for my mum and dad. Amen.

16

'You know, if you just set out to be liked, you would
be prepared to compromise on anything, wouldn't
you, at anytime? And you would achieve nothing!'

Margaret Thatcher, interview for Press Association,

3 May 1989

MY DAD SHOWS ME how to gamble. Cards and dice
are to him what bottles and cans are to my mum,
only he hides it better and sometimes wins.

I graduate from playing pontoon with him for pennies to
the Tossing where fistfuls of notes are won and lost. He takes
me for some overdue and uncomfortable father–son bonding
but I appreciate him making the effort. He doesn't bring
Teenie because it's not a place for girls (even though she's
starting to look more like a woman) and I'm not to tell her
about it and I don't – I love owning a bit of him that she
knows nothing about.

The Tossing is an illegal outdoor gambling circle. You get
there by bouncing along a country lane long after the road
runs out to a clearing hidden by giant chestnut trees. All the
cars park facing in so they can play into the night, their headlights on so they can still see the surprisingly shiny Victorian
pennies land. All depends on guessing the combination:
heads, tails or split. The same money just goes round and

round from hand to hand. Some men are forced to walk all the way home after losing their cars, time enough to make up an excuse for the wife. They accept their losses readily because they believe that one day they'll win it all back. Some do. Most don't. I sit on an engine-warm bonnet between two of my dad's pals and I couldn't be happier. One of them is a baker and he brings overly sweet seconds. It's all going well until I'm allowed to throw my first toss and one of my coins bounces off, never to be found. My dad doesn't take me back after that. I'm bad luck.

So anyway, I am taking a gamble now.

We're doing our UCCA forms and it feels like I am writing a letter to my future. Miss Campbell oversees the application process. I tell her I want to apply to Oxford, I want to be like Sebastian in *Brideshead*. She explains that if you choose Oxford you can't apply anywhere else. So it's there or nowhere.

'No,' she says. 'Oxford's not for you.'

I'd rather she slapped me. She also looks pained. Am I not clever enough? As my guidance teacher she has to approve my application so I can't just apply and lie. I can't even forge her signature because she signs every form herself and there are only a few pupils from Brannock High School applying anywhere anyway. No Sebastian for me, not even Charles Ryder. Maybe Adrian Mole. I am so shocked it doesn't occur to me to apply to Sussex.

I've already decided I'm going to study journalism. If Jennifer Hart wasn't enough, the midnight adventures of Kolchak the Night Stalker on BBC Two solving supernatural mysteries with the aid of a tape recorder, a typewriter and whirring spools of microfiche are. I want to tell and sell stories. I love politics, which seems like gossip on a national scale – *Spitting Image* is one of my favourite programmes, the long-nosed Maggie in a pinstripe suit my favourite puppet. There aren't many journalism degrees but the BA at Napier University in Edinburgh is my top choice. My mum still dreams about me being a doctor so I've told her I'm applying for medicine at Aberdeen. She believes me. She still believes Heather is my girlfriend. She's not been to a parents' night for years – my dad's never been – and the school doesn't ask questions because I get good grades.

In my UCCA statement I highlight my experience as Captain of ALL the school quiz teams, including Young Consumer; debating and public speaking; my leading role in the Save *Eldorado* Campaign (I wrote to *Points of View* and organised petitions to keep the doomed BBC soap going because I fancied Marcus Tandy); and my directorship at Young Enterprise. I do it all with semicolons.

Me and Heather passed Higher English and we're sitting the CSYS exam – the last hurdle before uni. Mrs Kennedy bustles into the English staff room with our creative writing portfolios under her arm. She turns to me first. After six years of straight As I expect only praise. I have submitted a poem called 'Snake Eyes' about a man who stakes everything on one roll of the dice, one look from another man across the table, which transmits a signal only he can decode. I dare Mrs Kennedy to call my bluff.

'I won't let you submit this,' she says, dropping my poem on the table.

'Why?' I dare her.

'Because, because, I wouldn't want your grade to be affected by . . . maybe you should discuss this with Miss Campbell.'

This thought terrifies me because I care what Miss Campbell thinks. She and Mrs Shaw have become my friends, well, as much as teachers can be friends. At lunchtime, me and Heather and Scott McAlmont, John Jackson, Sonia Morrison and the other geeks hang out in Mrs Shaw's computer room even though only Scott is taking her class. Sometimes Mark joins us. The BBC Micros gather dust in a corner while we fight over whose turn it is to play Lemmings on the new IBM. So long as we bin our cans and crisp bags Mrs Shaw is happy to give us our own space away from the foyer. Sometimes she comes back five minutes before the break is up to laugh along with our gossip, always careful to wag a finger when we take the piss out of a staff member, while memorising our jokes to cackle with Miss Campbell. A couple of times each term they take me and Heather out for pizza to DiMaggio's in Hamilton and we reveal our hopes and fears for uni. We have garlic bread and bottomless colas and their full attention. It feels impossibly grown-up.

'How are things at home?' Miss Campbell always asks, knowing they're always terrible.

I just nod. When Mum and Dodger have given each other black eyes yet again and I'm seriously considering phoning social services and getting us taken into care, I say, 'not great.' Me and Teenie often discuss running away but decide it's better to stay together, stick it out, because we'll escape soon enough.

In addition to Miss Campbell and Mrs Shaw we have one more friend on the staff. Miss Walsh is barely older than us sixth years. She's fresh out of teacher training and is doing her first year of professional practice at Brannock High School. Her fringe, like her job, is new and she's still getting used to both. Waist-length hair the colour of Galaxy chocolate that my mum wouldn't put up with washing falls over freckled shoulders that are always bare. She drapes little cardigans around them like Sandy in *Grease*. Too young to be staff and too old to be a pupil, she is stuck between worlds. She sees that we're older than our years but younger than her supposed peers and joins us in the computer room. We let her. I'm taller than her, can get my arm round her shoulders as she proves one day when she pops up in my armpit.

Heather hates her. 'She's always blowing her fringe out her eyes and she looks at you.'

After a couple of weeks Miss Walsh – call me Michelle – asks if I want to go out after school.

'I'll bring Heather,' I nod. 'And Mark.'

'No.' She lays her hand on my forearm and it's small and warm. It's also red and flaky, scalded-looking. She pulls it back. 'Just you and me. I want to talk.'

I'm too flattered to question why she doesn't want my friends around. I tell Heather I've got an extra shift at the New Lotus. I feel guilty but excited when Michelle picks me up from the bottom of my road in her red Ford Fiesta. I want to know what she wants to talk to me about.

'We're going to the pictures,' she says. 'In Glasgow.'

The orange lights flash familiar overhead and I remind myself I'm not going to Bennett's. On the way Michelle tells me all about her husband and I'm shocked to learn she's married so young but she's Catholic, as I guessed from the name and the freckles. He's a bully and he doesn't understand her. I reach over to the gearstick and pat her hand. The stress has given her eczema, she says. I know all about bullies. We arrive at the newly opened Forge Shopping Centre and Multiplex near Celtic Football Ground at Parkhead. It's all glass pyramids and steel. 'For the yuppies,' my dad says, even though the yuppies are dying out in the recession down South. 'The money folk.'

'What do you want to see?' she asks, getting out her purse.

There's only one film I'm interested in and it's not a horror but I am terrified of seeing it: *Philadelphia*.

We sit in the front row in the dark and I watch Tom Hanks slowly die of AIDS and when it gets to the opera bit I'm bawling and she offers her breast for me to lay my head on and I'm worried I'll stain her nice creamy blouse.

Back in the car I dry my eyes and she goes on about her husband more and all I can think is: I'm going to die of AIDS. Maybe she thinks my sadness is for her. We stop at the bottom of my street and she jerks the handbrake on with surprising strength. Her hand wanders on to my leg. It's doing no harm so I leave it there. Her husband thinks she's having an affair. He checks up on her. She wishes she had a more sensitive man in her life. I nod a lot. The windows are steaming up. Suddenly her hand, her flaky red hand, is on my face, caressing my tear-smoothed cheek. She leans in and I smell popcorn on her breath as she opens her mouth and I manage to say 'No' and open the door and more or less fall out. I slam it behind me but open it again just as fast and she looks hopeful and I say, 'Thanks for the film,' and run round the corner and burst into the house panting.

'What's wrong?' says my mum, unusually sober.

What's wrong? Everything is wrong. But I can't tell her that. So I tell her about Miss Walsh instead and she's on the top step before I can stop her but the red car is long gone.

'Did she touch you?' my mum demands. She repeats the

question and stares at my crotch and I cover myself with my hands.

'Yes,' I say and start crying again for the film, for my doomed future. 'No!'

My mum is raging and that makes me feel loved: how could I ever have doubted her? 'Harlot!' she curses. 'Hoor. Touchin' ma laddie. Wait till I get into that school in the morning. I'll leave her without a name!'

But my mum doesn't phone Brannock High. That night Dodger kicks off and they end up fighting and when she remembers to ask me about it the next morning I am super vague, change my story. I think about telling Miss Campbell and Mrs Shaw but I don't want to get into trouble. Michelle asks me to go out to her car at lunchtime. As soon as the doors are closed she puts her hand on my arm and I shake it off. You'd think I'd slapped her. I tell her she has to leave me alone. I talk about appropriate behaviour and boundaries and don't let her get a word in. She says she doesn't understand and I talk about involving the police. I say I'll tell her husband we've been having an affair. She turns whiter than a school shirt on the first day of term. After that she doesn't try to hang out with us again. She finishes her placement a term early. I think of Sandy ending the prime of Miss Jean Brodie. It feels good.

Miss Walsh is on my mind as I take the incriminating poem to Miss Campbell. I sit opposite her in her guidance room and remember the time I went to her not long after I'd tried and failed with Jacqueline Slattery. Before I could say anything she told me about something called Clause 28, said she wanted to help but was legally prevented from promoting homosexuality. Clause 28 doesn't matter now because I'm not here for help, I'm beyond help. On the wall is the poster of the whirling merry-go-round on Brighton Pier and I wish I was riding one of the horses round and round for ever.

Miss Campbell reads my poem silently but her face says everything. 'Right,' she says. 'I agree with Mrs Kennedy. You can't submit this.'

'Why?' I ask. 'I mean, you're a maths teacher.'

'That doesn't matter. It's just . . . Damian, it's too . . . personal.'

The guidance room is a torture chamber of the unsaid. I know and she knows and neither of us dares say it out loud because then it'll be true.

'Miss,' I say, formalising this moment. 'I think I'm gay.'

She puts the poem down slowly and sits up as straight as she can in these low-slung chairs.

'You think?'

'I know.'

'No,' she says, as if denying me permission to go to the toilet. 'You're not.'

'Yes, I am.'

'And what about Heather?'

'Heather knows,' I explain. 'She doesn't care.'

'She should care. I care. This is not what I wanted for you, Damian. This is going to make your life very difficult, more difficult than it already is. I, you . . . just no.'

I explain that I've got no choice, there's nothing I can do, I want to change but I can't. I've tried. I start to cry.

Her face is set. It's a face I've seen before when she's about to suspend a problem pupil. I've broken no school rules. There's no punishment for her to dish out. Nothing she can say or do will change anything. So she stands up and opens the door.

'Out, I don't want to hear any more about it.'

I run straight to Mrs Shaw who is typing away in the computer room. Nothing can stop me now I've said it out loud. I feel freed up by the telling, unburdened. She is kinder, says Miss Campbell is just worried, only wants the best for me, and I realise they've already anticipated this, discussed it. I tell her I'm going to tell my mum, I'm going to tell everybody, I'm never going to lie about myself again. She cuddles me then holds me at arm's length and looks at me hard and wishes me luck.

I turn the poem in. I win the gamble. I get my A.

I have always relied on the kindness of teachers.

17

'I am extraordinarily patient, provided I get my own
way in the end.'

Margaret Thatcher, *Observer*, 4 April 1989

I T'S THE 12TH OF October 2009. I am now thirty-three
years old. I've made it to Brighton where I live with my
own Mr Hart and our pet chickens. It's sunglasses and scarf
weather and I'm sitting on the pebbly beach opposite the
Grand Hotel. TV crews are rehearsing spontaneous remarks
for their reports on the twenty-fifth anniversary of the
Brighton bombing. The sky is obediently Tory blue. The sea
dazzles with dancing sun pennies. I still can't believe I really
live here.

Walking along the seafront I smell the Grand before I see
it. Chlorine floats up from the swimming pool in the base-
ment, wafting through the revolving doors with the scent of
gingerbread biscuits being laid on complimentary tea-trays
and the faint hint of beeswax from parquet floors walked on
by the well-heeled.

You can easily identify room 629 where the timer deto-
nated at 2.54 a.m. on 12 October 1984. It came from a VHS
recorder just like the one me and Teenie used to watch at my
dad's. The bomb's room no longer has a balcony. It stands out
like a black tooth in an otherwise perfect smile.

Famous for needing fiendishly little sleep, Maggie was still awake in her suite (the aptly named 'Napoleon') when the bomb went off. She was probably working on her big speech for the next day, which was also her birthday, and I like to imagine she allowed some small bit of herself to get excited about that. What *exactly* was she doing right then? Looking up from her notes out to the watery blackness? Eyeing the whisky decanter? In that explosive moment five people were killed and thirty-four seriously injured but she was completely unharmed. Minutes after the blast she emerged, Terminator-like, from the rubble with dust clouds billowing around her. I watched it all in black-and-white on the portable telly in that flat in Carfin.

Looking merely mildly inconvenienced as she left the half-destroyed hotel, Maggie paused to give a determined interview to the BBC: 'You hear about these atrocities . . . you don't expect them to happen to you . . . life must go on as usual.'

Indeed, it must. Does. Has.

It's too many years since I've visited Mark or Heather, since our secret nights out dancing at Bennett's. Life in Brighton is busy. Most days I commute into London to whatever paper I'm working on and most evenings I arrive home late, the express from Victoria rarely all that express. Mrs Hart never had to take public transport.

My last visit to Scotland changed my life. I was at Lancaster University studying English literature and sociology but wanted to get even further from home, so far it would stop being home for ever. The English department offered a scholarship to the University of Texas at Austin. I went for the interview without even looking at an atlas and got it.

They covered travel and tuition but I needed something to live on. I rang my old teachers Miss Campbell and Mrs Shaw and they put the word out to their friends. Within a week I was summoned back to Brannock for a meeting with a lawyer. His name was Mr Brown.

'Just be yourself,' Miss Campbell said, showing me into the headmaster's office.

Mr Brown looked like a friendly vicar in a pinstripe suit. 'Sit down,' he said, from behind Mr Margrave's desk. I looked around, never having been bad enough to be summoned here.

'So, Mr Barr, how much do you need?' he asked, reading over my CV.

'Sorry?'

'How much do you need?'

'Don't you want to know what I need it for? Or make sure I actually deserve it?' I laughed nervously, wishing I hadn't worn denim dungarees.

'You're eighteen,' said Mr Brown. 'I am sure you'll find ways to spend my client's money and that at least some of them,' he peered over his half-moon specs, 'will be wise.'

'I need £5,000,' a sum twice my student grant and more than I could imagine.

'My client will give you £10,000.'

He was already writing a cheque. I couldn't believe it.

'Thank you –' I started.

'Don't thank me,' interrupted Mr Brown, already putting the lid back on his fountain pen. 'Thank my client.'

'But who is your client?'

'My client wishes to remain anonymous. All he asks is that you write him a letter each term relating your progress. It is a specific condition of his gift that you do not even attempt to find out who he is. Understood?'

I nodded and stood. I almost bowed. He handed me the cheque and it didn't turn to air and I thanked him again, turning to leave, my hand on the door handle.

'Do you have a girlfriend?'

I froze. No, I did not. But I did have a boyfriend. I remembered coming out to Heather, Miss Campbell, Mrs Shaw, my mum, my dad and everybody else. I looked down at my black-leather brogues, the ones my auntie Louisa gave me because she said I had a long hard road ahead. I promised never to lie again about who I was.

'No,' I said, without turning round. 'Why?'

'She'd miss you, that's all. Well, safe travels, Mr Barr.'

And so I went to Texas and when I got on the plane I tried to look like I did it all the time and turned left not knowing there was a first class. The stewardess let me stay. Mr Brown is long dead but every now and then I write a letter to my mysterious benefactor. I've never had one back. I've travelled lots since then (never first class!). So has Heather. She taught English as a foreign language all around the world. We joke that all her pupils have a lovely Scottish accent. She's settled down near Worcester. I live here by the sea. Mark didn't make it to university. He was more than smart enough but it wasn't for him, he said. He got a job as a care assistant instead. He's still in Scotland.

Mobile phone reception is patchy on Brighton beach but a couple of bars of signal blow in from the sea and I get through to Heather and we agree that yes, it's been far too long, and arrange a visit for the following week. I always leave Brighton reluctantly and every time I get on the train I feel a flutter of panic, a seagull caught in a sudden gust of wind. As I board the intercity to Glasgow I remind myself I'm not fourteen and being forced back to Scotland after losing the Young Consumer Quiz final. The sea will be waiting for me when I get back. It will.

This train feels faster than usual and soon, almost too soon, I arrive at Motherwell Station and there she is, leaning on the old navy-blue Cavalier she got from Mrs D. It's years since I've seen her, two or three at least. It's a whole decade since me and her and Mark were last here together. Apart from the fact she's finally opted for a fringe, Heather looks just the same as the day Mark dared me to throw a milkshake on her legs. We cuddle and for a moment I think how things might have been different and she smiles when I explain the flowers I'm carrying are for Mark, not her.

'Of course they are,' she says. 'I'll drive.'

We joke about how her dad's eyes would vibrate out their sockets if he caught me behind the wheel. I've written off two cars (and counting). 'You're too easily distracted,' she says, mirror then signal then manoeuvre.

I've told my family I'm coming. My mum's had my old room ready for weeks and Teenie has changed her shift at the hospital and Billy is taking a day off. All for the prodigal son. Dodger is long gone so my dad might drop in. I'll take Heather home for my mum's burnt offering. We start trading news about everybody we know or knew. I tell her I got an email from a pal in Glasgow about Big Jinty – she lost an arm after catching a skin infection on a sunbed but she's still a bouncer on the door at Bennett's. Heather nearly crashes laughing. This is the gory gossip we love, Glasgow gothic.

Soon we're coming up to the Craig only it's not there. There are no cooling towers puffing clouds into the sky, no massive factories, no giant diggers. Even the great steel gates, padlocked for ever in 1992, are gone.

'Where's the Craig?'

Heather studied geography. This is the sort of thing she knows.

'Gone,' she says, dry as ever, gesturing with one hand as if she made it disappear.

'I can see that.'

Echoes of the protest. 'MAGGIE! MAGGIE! MAGGIE! OUT! OUT! OUT!' Maggie's broken promise. All those men. My dad's last shift.

They've even taken all the old soil away – toxic, they say. Soon there will be a college, a sports centre, a call centre and some affordable housing. The Craig is being regenerated, forgotten. There's only one sunset now.

Heather motors up the brae through Carfin. It takes some effort but I stare at Flat 1, 1 Magdalene Drive – my eyes find my old bedroom window now double glazed with white plastic frames. My mum's handrail still guards the steps and it's surprisingly shiny. A man who looks like Kev pushes a double buggy.

'And where's the Sippy?' I ask with a mock outrage that's not totally mock. All this progress in my past without my permission.

'Stop asking me like I've done something with them!'

All those acres of powdery chalk are gone, blown away maybe, covered by hundreds of Barratt boxes in neat ranks.

'It was technically a brownfield site,' says Heather.

They'll never know what went on in their foundations.

Carfin quickly turns into Newarthill and now we're passing Keir Hardie. I remember the Polaroid that Mr Baker took of me and Mark and Brian on our last day at primary school. I wonder where it is now. I know where Brian is. He drowned aged eighteen at a party on a loch; his funeral was our first and only class reunion. Me and him were the last to learn to swim.

'Do you want to go in and see Miss Campbell and Mrs Shaw?' I ask Heather as we approach Brannock.

'Nah,' she says. 'They'll be teaching.'

'We could go in and make sure nobody's scrubbed our names off the Dux board.'

'I'm sure we're still up there.'

We roll past Brannock, talking mad fast rubbish, our accents reverting to type, beyond type. We do our best to sound worse than the 'worstest' Rab C. Nesbitt character, shouting 'Haw hen' and 'See you, ya bam!' We camp it up and laugh more than we should. The houses they built over the Bing look like they've always been there now. I wonder if the frogs still find their way back.

Leaving Newarthill we go down through New Stevenson past Granny Barr's old house. Granpa Barr died years ago and didn't get a good turnout. At his funeral I shook hands with cousins, uncles and an aunt I'd not seen for decades. At the tea after there was nothing savoury, not a single sandwich – only tiers and tiers of puffs and fancies.

'He's no here to stop me now,' said Granny Barr, her cake-round face powdered with icing sugar. Diabetes got her not long after.

A few doors down is Logan's mother's house. She's dead too but he's in there. I check my seatbelt to make sure it's on.

Heather says nothing, just pats my hand. A couple of years ago Logan got jumped. They actually kicked his head in and now he carries around an aneurysm. Tick, tock. He can't even race his pigeons in case the excitement makes it blow. The police never caught the men that did it. He won't be getting a good turnout.

'Wit's fur yae, disnae go by ye,' I say.

'Get you, Granny Mac,' says Heather, indicating left. We drive on in silence for a bit. Soon she slows to a stop. Mirror, signal, manoeuvre.

'Don't forget Mark's flowers,' she says, tightening the hand-brake.

I see him now – blue eyes straight ahead, toes edging over the highest diving board, fearless. Determined. Mark had been trying for years – slashing his wrists or taking pills then promising not to do it again. He couldn't see a way to be happy. He couldn't see a way to be him. Not long after we both turned twenty-three he took one last leap into the unknown – hanged himself. His mother and father each insisted on installing a headstone on his grave. Neither reveals how or why their only son is down there. At the funeral I was asked to give a eulogy. His stepmother, the hated Grotbags, insisted on reading it beforehand. She handed my notes back with whole chunks scrubbed out. I nodded solemnly and stepped up to the lectern, taking an uncensored version from my inside pocket and reading it anyway, watching their faces turn white as I talked about how much I loved Mark, how he struggled to be gay in a world of bigots, how I would miss my Sister. Heather beamed at me through tears from the front row of the church.

Grotbags cornered me outside. 'I blame three things for him being in that coffin: his mother, Madonna and YOU!' Mark would have loved it.

I am the only boy still alive in Mr Baker's Polaroid. *Make-da-da,* Mark. You and me us never part. Never.

Be strong, Maggie told us all. Get educated. Get away. That's what she said. I listened. Heather listened. Mark didn't.

One November afternoon at Brannock High School, Mr Roebuck pushes the telly through the door of modern studies like a surgeon rushing a patient into theatre. He slams it on and his urgency shuts us all up. Maggie is standing outside 10 Downing Street and Denis is waiting behind, as always. Why is she not wearing her usual blue? She thanks us all even though nobody watching here voted for her. She says she's leaving the country a better place than she found it and the whole class laughs, me included. We jump out our seats and dance about and cheering erupts all over the school. Mr Roebuck shouts, 'She's gone!' when she sits in the back of the car and then, only then, does she start to cry. I stop cheering and sit down. Her eyes are red-rimmed like the big St Bernard next door to my dad. I feel sorry for her. Then I feel guilty for feeling sorry.

Yes, Maggie, you snatched all the milk and sent my teachers out to strike. Yes, you smashed the miners, closed the Craig and took away our second sunset. Yes, you made millions unemployed then cut their benefits. Yes, you shut down the mental hospitals and landed my already mad house with crazy Auntie Cat. Yes, you privatised gas and electricity so we ended up with a hungry meter, going to bed with clothes on so we didn't have to dress for school in the cold.

Yes, you created Clause 28 to 'prohibit the teaching of homosexuality', which wasn't very successful in my case. Yes, you devised the Poll Tax so I got the most exciting moddies lesson ever thanks to Tommy Sheridan. Yes, you gave me choices when I needed chances.

Yes, you did all that.

You also saved my life.

You were different, like me, and you had to fight to be yourself. You were the only woman among all those men. You fought wars and won them, even managing to carry off a headscarf at the helm of a tank. You led by example. You made a hero of the individual, a cult of the striver and I did my homework to impress you. I was greedy for more, devouring books and turning myself into an appreciating machine. You made that greed good. You created Channel 4, which showed me my first gay kiss. You hated where I was from and I did too so you made it OK for me to run away and never look back. You offered me certainty, however grim, when I had none at home. You threw me an escape ladder.

You made it possible – but not probable – for me to be the man I am now. Today you can often be found in one of the smaller Central London parks, walking slowly, oh-so-slowly on the arm of a paid companion like a dowager aunt from P.G. Wodehouse. Your head is bent now: a symptom of your malady, history weighing heavily, maybe just all that hairspray. Your perfect do has morphed from a platinum Lego helmet to a gentle champagne-coloured halo. Few people passing would guess you were once the most powerful woman in the world. I want to come to that park and watch you. I don't want to talk to you or trouble you. I want to see you in person just once before you go.

My other mother.

I want to watch you walk through the world before you leave it and if you stumble I'll rush forward to catch you. I like to think I'd show you the kindness you never showed me. I'd like you to owe me a favour. I want to show you that I did it. I want you to be proud of me.

EPILOGUE

THE ATHENAEUM IS THE most exclusive of London's private member clubs. I am here to interview a retired senior civil servant – who I'll call Sir Humphrey – for a feature I'm working on. 'Be sure to wear a tie,' he reminds me in an email. There's no need for such a reminder, the arriviste is always alert to any code. I arrive fifteen minutes early and as usual feel like I'm infiltrating.

Sir Humphrey is twinkly-eyed and more energetic than I'd imagined. His tie is unexpectedly red. Waiters pull our chairs out and in that ritual act of faith we trust them not to take revenge on us by leaving them there when we fall back. The menu is grand and ordering is byzantine, Cunard cruise liner *circa* 1925. I am not allowed to address the staff directly. Sir Humphrey asks what I'd like and I tell him and he tells the waiter, who fills out a form. The food arrives surprisingly swiftly and our interview begins. But soon, very soon, we veer off-course. Sir Humphrey saw Maggie every day, she brushed past him in her tight-boned corsets, watched everything he did.

'She changed my life the day I met her,' he says, taking a pat of butter and smearing it on his side plate before breaking a bread roll in his hands.

I watch him and copy. She changed my life the day I met her too, on the telly, walking away from that bomb.

Soon I forget my questions. Sir Humphrey eats little as he talks almost constantly for the next four hours leaving only official gaps for official secrets. He tells me how Maggie toured her new kingdom immediately after winning and plucked him from relative obscurity in one of the many departments she didn't trust.

'The next Monday I was in Downing Street.' Like her, he was a grammar school exception. 'The Old Etonians called her the Pound Coin: "thick and brassy and thinks she's a sovereign". She was like an empress bestowing favour and exacting punishment.'

Lunch is turning into afternoon tea. Neither of us wants to leave. Having completed its time travel a rum baba arrives for pudding.

Finally, as the coffee cups are cleared away, Sir Humphrey leans towards me. 'I don't know how you'll feel about this,' he says, almost whispering in the now empty dining room. 'But she would have liked you, you know.'

'Me?' I am aware I sound too loud. I lay my spoon down quietly.

'Yes,' he says appraisingly. 'You. I think she would have liked you very much indeed.'

ACKNOWLEDGEMENTS

Writing this book has been an extension of living – and reliving – my life. For years, whenever I tried to write something longer than a newspaper feature, I kept returning to my own story – fragments, details, feelings. The sort of stuff you get out of your system and put in a drawer and forget. That drawer is now very full and securely locked, I'm pleased to say.

This self-indulgence was frustrating – surely I had better stories to tell than my own. I felt it signified a lack of imagination. I was right. Almost all of what I wrote was mortifying but somewhere in there was a voice, my own. I listened hard for a long time and among the shouts and whispers I finally heard it. I needed to remember, not imagine. This was not always easy.

The first person to hear this echo was Clare Conville – my agent and my friend. She saw something in embarrassing early efforts and her stylish combination of criticism, encouragement and martinis turned pages into a proposal and then a manuscript and now a book. She introduced me to Louisa Joyner, whose early editorial thoughts were invaluable. Thank you both and to all at Conville & Walsh especially all the Alexes.

Bloomsbury was my dream publisher and what a dream! Alexandra Pringle has inspired and terrified in equal measure, holding my book to her standards. I couldn't have a better editor. Line-by-line and page-by-page I've been accompanied by the tireless Gillian Stern who somehow matches sensitivity and thoroughness. David Mann is responsible for the jacket, which I love more and more every time I see it. Thank you also to Alexa, Maria, Alice, Oliver, Mary and Sarah.

'There is no point in describing experience unless you try to get it as near to being what it really was as you can make it,' wrote Diana Athill. 'Get it right,' she said to me. I've tried my very best to follow her advice and I'm grateful to her for that and much, much more.

My Literary Salon at Shoreditch House allows me to share ideas, and cocktails, with incredible writers. I'm thankful to them all for inspiring me and especially: Jake Arnott, Louis de Bernières, Chris Cleave, John Crace, Geoff Dyer, Helen Fielding, James Frey, Patrick Gale, Janice Galloway, Richard Holloway, Howard Jacobson, Andrew Miller, David Mitchell, Maggie O'Farrell, D.B.C. Pierre, Alex Preston, Rupert Thomson, Colm Tóibín and John Waters (for telling me how to sign a colostomy bag – should I ever be asked to). Thanks, of course, to Russell Finch, Nick Jones, Dan Flower, Vanessa and all at Shoreditch House and all the fabulous Salonistas! And to Peter Hutton – the world's best assistant.

Thank you to the following friends for being kind and brave enough to read very early on: Naomi Alderman, Caz Biss, Brian Halley, Alexandra Heminsley, Henry Jeffreys, Eleanor 'cousin' Moran, David Nicholls, Jess Ruston and Sister Sophia. Particular gratitude to Polly Samson and David Gilmour not just for reading and thinking and caring but also for taking in my wayward chickens. Feathered thanks to all my Girls.

For encouragement, cocktails and kindness: Alex Bellos, Ella Berthoud, Susie Boyt, Sally Chatterton, Jessica Fellowes, Max Ginnane, Katy Guest, Anoushka Healey, Liz Hoggard, Richard Holloway, Nick Ib, India Knight, Jonathan Lee, Sam Leith, Stephanie Merrit, Kirsty Milner, Jojo Moyes, Tiffany Murray, Rowan Pelling, Dotson Rader, Ann Siegel, Sathnam Sanghera, Craig Taylor, Shaun and Polly at Tilton House, Janice Turner, S.J. Watson and Zoe Williams. Thank you all. This round is on me!

Lucy Aitkens, Neil Byrne, Joshua van der Broek, Sham and Clive, Rob Kendrick, Simon Lock, Eileen and Bertie Maccabe, Jeff Melnyk, Bakul Patki, Iram Quraishi and Ruthe Waineman have all put up with my endless book blethering. Thank you for listening lovingly. Now, what was I saying?

Much of this book was written at Aikwood Tower in the Scottish Borders. It's almost intimidatingly inspiring. I'm very grateful to Rory and Vicky Steel for their generous hospitality and to Roddy for caretaking me.

Of all the things I've written this feels the most important – not because it's all about me. Yes, it's a memoir but my story is shared. I've done my very best to be careful with and faithful to all the people you've met. Names have been changed. Some things have been forgotten. Some things can't be. You've read it so you know and they do too. I am most grateful to my mum, dad, sister and brother and to Miss Campbell, Mrs Shaw, Heather and Mark (wherever he is now).

And, of course, Maggie.

A Note on Milk Snatching

'Thatcher, Thatcher, Milk Snatcher' will follow Maggie to her grave. It is true that she ended free school milk for all over sevens in 1971 when she was Education Secretary under Edward Heath. Until then every pupil under eighteen was entitled to a third of a pint a day under the Free Milk Act introduced in 1946 by another pioneering woman, Ellen Wilkinson, the first female education minister (Labour). Despite Thatcher's cuts many local education authorities continued providing free milk and in 1977 the EEC School Milk Subsidy Scheme was introduced. If, like me, you got free school meals you continued to get free school milk – this remains true today.